Python For Busy People

Designed for Busy People with Deadlines

Derrick Cassidy

Python For Busy People

Designed for Busy People with Deadlines

Derrick Cassidy

This is a Leanpub book. Leanpub empowers authors and publishers with the Lean Publishing process. Lean Publishing is the act of publishing an in-progress ebook using lightweight tools and many iterations to get reader feedback, pivot until you have the right book and build traction once you do.

I would like to thank my wife Uka for putting up with my long hours while writing this book. Also I would like thank my parents for always being supportive in my endeavors as always and I love you both with all my heart.

Contents

Introduction

You have taken the first step to learning Python 3 by purchasing "**Python For Busy People**". This book was designed with the novice Python programmer and/or information technology professional who doesn't have programming experience, but wants or needs to learn Python to do jobs or tasks related to the programming language. If you need to learn Python for tasks such as data scrubbing, network automation, web development, etc., this is the book for you.

In my personal experience, I had to learn Python to analyze data sets from CSV files and excel spreadsheets using Pandas[1]. With Pandas for example, it is important to learn about Python functions, classes, lists, sets, and dictionaries to name a few, to clean raw data sets to make the data useful for data analysis.

If you are a Network Engineer, or work in other information technology disciplines, there is a high possibility that you had to pull APIs (Application Programming Interfaces) from external data sources (i.e. outside of your company or client's network) needed for things like internal audit purposes as an example. If this sounds like you this is the right book for you. This text will get you on the right track to learning the essentials of the Python programming language. Python has become the programming language of choice for many day to day IT tasks, in many companies globally. One of the many reasons that Python have been used by some many IT departments is Python is powerful. The Python language is expressive and productive, with a "batteries included" approach packaged with a extensive standard library[2] as well as a plethora of third-party libraries[3]. With Python you can build simple scripts to complex applications. This book will not make you an expert in the Python programming language, but it will provide you with the foundations to do day-to-day tasks in a IT environment.

---

[1]https://pandas.pydata.org/
[2]https://docs.python.org/3/library/index.html
[3]https://pypi.org/

Overview

This book comprises of 35 sections (not including the introduction and this overview sections). The sections was design to be concise and get to the point of the Pythonic syntax and concepts, without getting too bogged down with theory on the "why" but on the "how".

By the end of the book you'll have learned the foundations and the fundamentals of the Python 3.x programming language. You will learn the language elements, features and libraries (i.e. Python build-in standard library), with hundreds of examples throughout the book to reinforce your learning. Reading alone will not help you learn Python, but coding out the examples in this texts will give you the retention and confidence to begin coding your own scripts and programs. I encourage you to experiment with your own code examples, as you work your way to the end of the book. This will increase your success in not just mechanical learning, but conceptualize the core concepts of the Python programming language.

The Sections are:

1. Python Syntax
2. Python Comments
3. Python Variables
4. Python Data Types
5. Python Numbers
6. Python Casting
7. Python Strings
8. Python Booleans
9. Python Operators
10. Python Lists
11. Python Tuples
12. Python Sets
13. Python Dictionaries
14. Python If...Else
15. Python While Loops
16. Python For Loops
17. Python Functions
18. Python Lambda
19. Python Arrays
20. Python Classes/Objects
21. Python Inheritance
22. Python Iterators
23. Python Polymorphism

Python Syntax

Section 1: Syntax

Section 1.1 - Execution of Python Syntax

Python syntax can be executed by writing directly in the command line:

```
1  >>> print("Hello, Python!")
2  Hello, Python!
```

You can also execute a Python file from the command line, using the `.py` file extension, and running it, as in the example below:

```
1  C:\Users\Your Name>python myfile.py
```

Section 1.2 - Python Indentation

Indentation in Python refers to the spaces at the beginning of a code line.

Where in other programming languages the indentation in code is for readability only, the indentation in Python is very important.

Python uses indentation to indicate a block of code as in the example below:

```
1  if 7 > 3:
2    print("Seven is greater than three.")
```

The Python interpreter will throw an error if you don't include the indentation in a code block when required, as in the example below:

```
1  if 7 > 3:
2  print("Seven is greater than three.")
```

The common practice among the Python community is to use four spaces, but it has to have at least one space, or the Python interpreter will throw an error.

Section 1.3 - Python Variables

In Python, variables are created when you assign a value to it using the assignment operator =, as in the examples below :

```
1   first_name = "Johnny"
2   last_name = "Appleseed"
3   age = 25
```

Unlike many other programming languages, Python has no command for declaring a variable.

Section 1.4 - Python Comments

Python has commenting for the use of providing in-code documentation.

Comments start with the #, and Python will render the rest of the line as a comment, as in the example below:

```
1   # This is a comment line
2   print("Learning Python comments is fun.")
```

> **Note:** Unlike other programming languages, semicolons ; are not required at the end of a code statement in Python.

Python Comments

Section 2 : Comments

Section 2.1 - Comments

Below are reasons you will want to create comments in your codebase:

- Comments can be used to explain sections of your Python code.
- Comments can be used to make the codebase more readable.
- Comments can be used to prevent execution of code for testing purposes.

Section 2.2 - Creating a Comment

Comments start with the #, and Python will render the rest of the line as a comment, as in the example below:

```
1  # This is a comment line
2  print("Learning Python comments is fun.")
```

Comments can be placed at the end of a line, and Python will ignore the rest of the line, as in the example below:

```
1  print("Understanding comments in Python is important.") # This is a comment on the e\
2  nd of the statement
```

A comment does not have to be text that explains the code, it can also be used to prevent Python from executing code, as in the example below:

```
1  #print("It's raining in Spain.")
2  print("Today is sunny in New York City.")
```

Section 2.3 - Multiline Comments

Python does not have a syntax for multiline comments.

To add a multiline comment you could insert a # for each line, as in the example below:

```
1   #This is a comment
2   #written in
3   #more than just one line
4   print("Hello, Python!")
```

Or, not quite as intended, you can use a multiline string.

Since Python will ignore string literals that are not assigned to a variable, you can add a multiline string (triple quotes) in your code, and place your comment inside it:

```
1   """
2   This is a comment
3   written in
4   more than just one line
5   """
6   print("Hello, World!")
```

As long as the string is not assigned to a variable, Python will read the code, but then ignore it, and you have made a multiline comment.

Python Variables

Section 3 - Python Variables

Section 3.1 - Variables

Variables are containers for storing data values.

Section 3.1.1 - Creating Variables

Python has no command for declaring a variable.

A variable is created the moment you first assign a value to it.

```python
1  first_name = "Shawn"
2  last_name = "Smith"
3  print(first_name)
4  print(last_name)
```

Variables do not need to be declared with any particular *type*, and can even change type after they have been set.

```python
1  x = 10      # x is of type int
2  x = "Joseph" # x is now of type str
3  print(x)
```

Section 3.1.2 - Casting

If you want to specify the data type of a variable, this can be done with casting.

```python
1  x = str(15)   # x will be '15' a string
2  y = int(15)   # y will be 15 a integer
3  z = float(15) # z will be 15.0 a float
4  print(x)
5  print(y)
6  print(z)
```

Section 3.1.3 - Get the Type

You can get the data type of a variable with the type() function.

```
1  x = 15
2  y = "Joseph"
3  print(type(x))
4  print(type(y))
```

Section 3.1.4 - Single or Double Quotation Marks?

String variables can be declared either by using single or double quotes:

```
1  x = "Joseph"
2  # is the same as
3  x = 'Joseph'
4  x == x # returns True because both are the same
```

Section 3.1.5 - Case-Sensitive

Variable names are case-sensitive.

```
1  a = 10
2  A = "Susan"
3  # A will not overwrite a
4  print(a)
5  print(A)
```

Section 3.2 - Python - Variable Names

Section 3.2.1 - Variable Names

A variable can have a short name (like x and y) or a more descriptive name (age, carname, total_-volume). Rules for Python variables:

- A variable name must start with a letter or the underscore character _
- A variable name cannot start with a number
- A variable name can only contain alpha-numeric characters and underscores (A-z, 0-9, and _)
- Variable names are case-sensitive (age, Age and AGE are three different variables)
- A variable name cannot be any of the Python keywords (also called reserved words, e.g. print).

Below are examples of legal Python variable names:

```
1   firstname = "Jack"
2   first_name = "Jack"
3   _first_name = "Jack"
4   firstName = "Jack"
5   FIRSTNAME = "Jack"
6   firstname2 = "Jack"
```

Below are examples of illegal Python variable names:

```
1   2firstname = "Jack"
2   first-name = "Jack"
3   first name = "Jack"
```

> **Note**: Remember that variable names are case-sensitive.

Section 3.2.2 - Multi Words Variable Names

Variable names with more than one word can be difficult to read.

There are several techniques you can use to make them more readable:

Section 3.2.3 - Camel Case

Each word, except the first, starts with a capital letter:

```
1   myVarableName = "Jack"
```

Section 3.2.4 - Pascal Case

Each word starts with a capital letter:

```
1   MyVariableName = "Jack"
```

Section 3.2.5 - Snake Case

Each word is separated by an underscore character (_)

```
1   my_variable_name = "Jack"
```

Section 3.3 - Python Variables - Assigned to Multiple Values

Section 3.3.1 - Many Values to Multiple Variables

Python allows you to assign values to multiple variables in one line:

```
1  var_1, var_2, var_3 = "Spring", "Summer", "Fall"
2  print(var_1)
3  print(var_2)
4  print(var_3)
```

Note: Make sure the number of variables matches the number of values, or else you will get an error.

Section 3.3.2 - One Value to Multiple Variables

And you can assign the *same* value to multiple variables in one line:

```
1  a = b = c = "Winter"
2  print(a)
3  print(b)
4  print(c)
```

Section 3.3.3 - Unpack a Collection

If you have a collection of values in a list, tuple etc. Python allows you to extract the values into variables. This is called *unpacking*.

Below is an example on how to unpack a list:

```
1  seasons = ["Winter", "Spring", "Summer", "Fall"]
2  a, b, c, d = seasons
3  print(a)
4  print(b)
5  print(c)
6  print(d)
```

Section 3.4 - Python - Output Variables

Section 3.4.1 - Output Variables

The Python print() function is often used to output variables.

```
1  x = "Learning Python is fun!"
2  print(x)
```

In the print() function, you output multiple variables, separated by a comma:

```
1  x = "Learning Python"
2  y = "is"
3  z = "fun!"
4  print(x, y, z)
```

You can also use the + operator to output multiple variables:

```
1  x = "Learning Python "
2  y = "is "
3  z = "fun!"
4  print(x + y + z)
```

Notice the space character after `"Learning Python "` and `"is "`, without them the result would be "LearningPythonisfun!".

For numbers, the + character works as a mathematical operator:

```
1  x = 5
2  y = 10
3  print(x + y)
```

In the `print()` function, when you try to combine a string and a number with the + operator, Python will give you an error:

```
1  x = 5
2  y = "Jack"
3  print(x + y)
```

The best way to output multiple variables in the `print()` function is to separate them with commas, which even support different data types:

```
1  x = 5
2  y = "Jack"
3  print(x, y)
```

Section 3.5 - Python - Global Variables

Section 3.5.1 - Global Variables

Variables that are created outside of a function (as in all of the examples above) are known as global variables.

Global variables can be used by everyone, both inside of functions and outside.

In the example below, we create a variable outside of a function, and use it inside the function:

```
1  x = "fun!"
2
3  def myfunc():
4   print("Learning Python is " + x)
5
6  myfunc()
```

If you create a variable with the same name inside a function, this variable will be local, and can only be used inside the function. The global variable with the same name will remain as it was, global and with the original value.

In the example below, we create a variable inside a function, with the same name as the global variable:

```
1  x = "fun!"
2
3  def myfunc():
4   x = "awesome!"
5   print("Learning Python is " + x)
6
7  myfunc()
8
9  print("Learning Python is " + x)
```

Section 3.5.2 - The `global` Keyword

Normally, when you create a variable inside a function, that variable is local, and can only be used inside that function.

To create a global variable inside a function, you can use the `global` keyword.

If you use the `global` keyword, the variable belongs to the global scope:

```
1  def myfunc():
2   global x
3   x = "awesome!"
4
5  myfunc()
6
7  print("Python is " + x)
```

Also, use the `global` keyword if you want to change a global variable inside a function.

To change the value of a global variable inside a function, refer to the variable by using the `global` keyword:

```
1  x = "fun!"
2
3  def myfunc():
4    global x
5    x = "awesome!"
6
7  myfunc()
8
9  print("Learning Python is " + x)
```

Python Data Types

Section 4.1 - Built-in Data Types

In programming, data type is an important concept.

Variables can store data of different types, and different types can do different things.

Python has the following data types built-in by default, in these categories:

Text Type:	`str`
Numeric Types:	`int, float, complex`
Sequence Types:	`list, tuple, range`
Mapping Type:	`dict`
Set Types:	`set, frozenset`
Boolean Type:	`bool`
Binary Types:	`bytes, bytearray, memoryview`
None Type:	`NoneType`

Section 4.2 - Getting the Data Type

You can get the data type of any object by using the `type()` function:

Print the data type of the variable x:

```
1  x = 25
2  print(type(x))
```

Section 4.3 - Setting the Data Type

In Python, the data type is set when you assign a value to a variable:

Example	Data Type
x = "Hello World"	str
x = 20	int
x = 20.5	float
x = 1j	complex
x = ["apple", "banana", "cherry"]	list
x = ("apple", "banana", "cherry")	tuple
x = range(6)	range
x = {"name" : "John", "age" : 36}	dict
x = {"apple", "banana", "cherry"}	set
x = frozenset({"apple", "banana", "cherry"})	frozenset
x = True	bool
x = b"Hello"	bytes
x = bytearray(5)	bytearray
x = memoryview(bytes(5))	memoryview
x = None	NoneType

Section 4.4 - Setting the Specific Data Type

If you want to specify the data type, you can use the following constructor functions:

Example	Data Type
x = str("Hello World")	str
x = int(20)	int
x = float(20.5)	float
x = complex(1j)	complex
x = list(("apple", "banana", "cherry"))	list
x = tuple(("apple", "banana", "cherry"))	tuple
x = range(6)	range
x = dict(name="John", age=36)	dict
x = set(("apple", "banana", "cherry"))	set
x = frozenset(("apple", "banana", "cherry"))	frozenset
x = bool(5)	bool
x = bytes(5)	bytes
x = bytearray(5)	bytearray
x = memoryview(bytes(5))	memoryview

Python Numbers

Section 5.1 - Numbers

There are three numeric types in Python:

- int
- float
- complex

Variables of numeric types are created when you assign a value to them:

```
1   x = 1   # int
2   y = 2.8 # float
3   z = 1j  # complex
```

To verify the type of any object in Python, use the type() function:

```
1   print(type(x))
2   print(type(y))
3   print(type(z))
```

Section 5.1.1 - Int

Int, or integer, is a whole number, positive or negative, without decimals, of unlimited length.

Below are some examples of integers:

```
1   x = 1
2   y = 35656222554887711
3   z = -3255522
4
5   print(type(x))
6   print(type(y))
7   print(type(z))
```

Section 5.1.2 - Float

Float, or "floating point number" is a number, positive or negative, containing one or more decimals.

Below are some examples of floats:

```
1  x = 1.10
2  y = 1.0
3  z = -35.59
4
5  print(type(x))
6  print(type(y))
7  print(type(z))
```

Float can also be scientific numbers with an "e" to indicate the power of 10.

Below are some examples of numbers with scientific numbers:

```
1  x = 35e3
2  y = 12e4
3  z = -87.7e100
4
5  print(type(x))
6  print(type(y))
7  print(type(z))
```

Section 5.1.3 - Complex

Complex numbers are written with a "j" as the imaginary part:

Below are some examples of complex numbers:

```
1  x = 3 + 5j
2  y = 5j
3  z = -5j
4
5  print(type(x))
6  print(type(y))
7  print(type(z))
```

Section 5.2 - Type Conversion

You can convert from one type to another with the int(), float(), and complex() methods:

Below are examples of converting from one type to another:

```
1   x = 1   # int
2   y = 2.8 # float
3   z = 1j  # complex
4
5   #convert from int to float:
6   a = float(x)
7
8   #convert from float to int:
9   b = int(y)
10
11  #convert from int to complex:
12  c = complex(x)
13
14  print(a)
15  print(b)
16  print(c)
17
18  print(type(a))
19  print(type(b))
20  print(type(c))
```

Note: You **cannot** convert complex numbers into another number type.

Section 5.3 - Random Number

Python does not have a random() function to make a random number, but Python has a built-in module called random that can be used to make random numbers:

Import the random module, and display a random number between 1 and 9:

```
1   import random
2
3   print(random.randrange(1, 10))
```

Python Casting

Section 6.1 - Specify a Variable Type

There may be times when you want to specify a type on to a variable. This can be done with casting. Python is an object-orientated language, and as such it uses classes to define data types, including its primitive types.

Casting in python is therefore done using constructor functions:

- `int()` - constructs an integer number from an integer literal, a float literal (by removing all decimals), or a string literal (providing the string represents a whole number)
- `float()` - constructs a float number from an integer literal, a float literal or a string literal (providing the string represents a float or an integer)
- `str()` - constructs a string from a wide variety of data types, including strings, integer literals and float literals

Below are some examples of type casting integers:

```
1  x = int(1)   # x will be 1
2  y = int(2.8) # y will be 2
3  z = int("3") # z will be 3
```

Below are some examples of type casting floats:

```
1  w = float(1)     # x will be 1.0
2  x = float(2.8)   # y will be 2.8
3  y = float("3")   # z will be 3.0
4  z = float("4.2") # w will be 4.2
```

Below are some examples of type casting strings:

```
1  x = str("s1") # x will be 's1'
2  y = str(2)    # y will be '2'
3  z = str(3.0)  # z will be '3.0'
```

Python Strings

Section 7.1 - Strings

Strings in python are surrounded by either single quotation marks, or double quotation marks.

`'hello'` is the same as `"hello"`.

You can display a string literal with the `print()` function:

```
1  print("Hello") # double quotes
2  print('Hello') # single quotes
```

Section 7.1.1 - Assign String to a Variable

Assigning a string to a variable is done with the variable name followed by an equal sign (=) and the string:

```
1  a = "Hello"
2  print(a)
```

Section 7.1.2 - Multiline Strings

You can assign a multiline string to a variable by using three quotes:

Below is an example of using three double quotes:

```
1  a = """There is nothing in the world so irresistibly
2  contagious as laughter and good humor."""
3  print(a)
```

Below is an example of using three single quotes:

```
1  a = '''There is nothing in the world so irresistibly
2  contagious as laughter and good humor.'''
3  print(a)
```

Section 7.1.3 - Strings are Arrays

Like many other popular programming languages, strings in Python are arrays of bytes representing unicode characters.

However, Python does not have a character data type, a single character is simply a string with a length of 1.

Square brackets can be used to access elements of the string.

Get the character at position 1 (remember that the first character has the position 0):

```
1  a = "Hello, Python!"
2  print(a[1]) # output 'e'
```

Section 7.1.4 - Looping Through a String

Since strings are arrays, we can loop through the characters in a string, with a for loop.

Loop through the letters in the word "banana":

```
1  for x in "banana":
2    print(x)
```

Section 7.1.5 - String Length

To get the length of a string, use the len() function.

The len() function returns the length of a string:

```
1  a = "Hello, World!"
2  print(len(a))
```

Section 7.1.6 - Check String

To check if a certain phrase or character is present in a string, we can use the keyword in.

Check if "free" is present in the following text:

```
1  txt = "The best things in life are free!"
2  print("free" in txt)
```

Use it in an if statement:

Print only if "free" is present:

```
1  txt = "The best things in life are free!"
2  if "free" in txt:
3   print("Yes, 'free' is present.")
```

Section 7.1.7 - Check if NOT

To check if a certain phrase or character is NOT present in a string, we can use the keyword not in.

Check if "expensive" is NOT present in the following text:

```
1  txt = "The best things in life are free!"
2  print("expensive" not in txt)
```

Use it in an if statement:

```
1  # print only if "expensive" is NOT present
2  txt = "The best things in life are free!"
3  if "expensive" not in txt:
4   print("No, 'expensive' is NOT present.")
```

Section 7.2 - Slicing Strings

Section 7.2.1 - Slicing

You can return a range of characters by using the slice syntax.

Specify the start index and the end index, separated by a colon, to return a part of the string.

Get the characters from position 2 to position 5 (not included):

```
1  b = "Hello, World!"
2  print(b[2:5]) # prints 'llo'
```

Note: The first character has index 0.

Section 7.2.2 - Slice From the Start

By leaving out the start index, the range will start at the first character:

Get the characters from the start to position 5 (not included):

```
1   b = "Hello, World!"
2   print(b[:5]) # prints 'Hello'
```

Section 7.2.3 - Slice To the End

By leaving out the *end* index, the range will go to the end:

Get the characters from position 2, and all the way to the end:

```
1   b = "Hello, World!"
2   print(b[2:]) # prints 'llo, World!'
```

Section 7.2.4 - Negative Indexing

Use negative indexes to start the slice from the end of the string:

Get the characters:

From: "o" in "World!" (position -5)

To, but not included: "d" in "World!" (position -2):

```
1   b = "Hello, World!"
2   print(b[-5:-2]) # prints 'orl'
```

Section 7.3 - Modify Strings

Python has a set of built-in methods that you can use on strings.

Section 7.3.1 - Upper Case

The upper() method returns the string in upper case:

```
1   a = "Hello, World!"
2   print(a.upper()) # prints 'HELLO, WORLD!'
```

Section 7.3.2 - Lower Case

The lower() method returns the string in lower case:

```
1  a = "Hello, World!"
2  print(a.lower()) # prints 'hello, world!'
```

Section 7.3.3 - Remove Whitespace

Whitespace is the space before and/or after the actual text, and very often you want to remove this space.

The strip() method removes any whitespace from the beginning or the end:

```
1  a = " Hello, World! " # notice the whitespace before/after the quotes.
2  print(a.strip()) # returns "Hello, World!" - whitespace removed.
```

Section 7.3.4 - Replace String

The replace() method replaces a string with another string:

```
1  a = "Hello, World!"
2  print(a.replace("H", "J")) # prints 'Jello, World!'
```

Section 7.3.5 - Split String

The split() method returns a list where the text between the specified separator becomes the list items.

The split() method splits the string into substrings if it finds instances of the separator:

```
1  a = "Hello, World!"
2  print(a.split(",")) # returns ['Hello', ' World!']
```

Section 7.4 - String Concatenation

String Concatenation

To concatenate, or combine, two strings you can use the + operator.

Merge variable a with variable b into variable c:

```
1  a = "Hello"
2  b = "World"
3  c = a + b
4  print(c)
```

To add a space between them, add a " ":

```
1  a = "Hello"
2  b = "World"
3  c = a + " " + b
4  print(c)
```

Section 7.5 - Format Strings

Section 7.5.1 - String Format

As we learned in the Python Variables chapter, we cannot combine strings and numbers like this:

```
1  age = 25
2  txt = "My name is Jack, I am " + age
3  print(txt)
```

But we can combine strings and numbers by using the `format()` method!

The `format()` method takes the passed arguments, formats them, and places them in the string where the placeholders `{}` are:

Use the `format()` method to insert numbers into strings:

```
1  age = 25
2  txt = "My name is Jack, and I am {}"
3  print(txt.format(age))
```

The `format()` method takes unlimited number of arguments, and are placed into the respective placeholders:

```
1  quantity = 3
2  itemno = 567
3  price = 49.95
4  myorder = "I want {} pieces of item {} for {} dollars."
5  print(myorder.format(quantity, itemno, price))
```

You can use index numbers {0} to be sure the arguments are placed in the correct placeholders:

```
1  quantity = 3
2  itemno = 567
3  price = 49.95
4  myorder = "I want to pay {2} dollars for {0} pieces of item {1}."
5  print(myorder.format(quantity, itemno, price))
```

Section 7.6 - Escape Characters

Section 7.6.1 - Escape Character

To insert characters that are illegal in a string, use an escape character.

An escape character is a backslash \ followed by the character you want to insert.

An example of an illegal character is a double quote inside a string that is surrounded by double quotes.

You will get an error if you use double quotes inside a string that is surrounded by double quotes:

```
1  txt = "We are the so-called "Vikings" from the north."  # throws an error
```

To fix this problem, use the escape character \":

The escape character allows you to use double quotes when you normally would not be allowed:

```
1  txt = "We are the so-called \"Vikings\" from the north."
```

Section 7.6.2 - Escape Characters

Other escape characters used in Python

Code	Result
\'	Single Quote
\\	Backslash
\n	New Line
\r	Carriage Return
\t	Tab
\b	Backspace
\f	Form Feed
\ooo	Octal value
\xhh	Hex value

Section 7.7 - String Methods

Python has a set of built-in methods that you can use on strings.

Note: All string methods return new values. They do not change the original string.

Method	Description
capitalize()	Converts the first character to upper case
casefold()	Converts string into lower case
center()	Returns a centered string
count()	Returns the number of times a specified value occurs in a string
encode()	Returns an encoded version of the string
endswith()	Returns true if the string ends with the specified value
expandtabs()	Sets the tab size of the string
find()	Searches the string for a specified value and returns the position of where it was found
format()	Formats specified values in a string
format_map()	Formats specified values in a string
index()	Searches the string for a specified value and returns the position of where it was found
isalnum()	Returns True if all characters in the string are alphanumeric
isalpha()	Returns True if all characters in the string are in the alphabet
isascii()	Returns True if all characters in the string are ascii characters
isdecimal()	Returns True if all characters in the string are decimals
isdigit()	Returns True if all characters in the string are digits
isidentifier()	Returns True if the string is an identifier

Method	Description
islower()	Returns True if all characters in the string are lower case
isnumeric()	Returns True if all characters in the string are numeric
isprintable()	Returns True if all characters in the string are printable
isspace()	Returns True if all characters in the string are whitespaces
istitle()	Returns True if the string follows the rules of a title
isupper()	Returns True if all characters in the string are upper case
join()	Joins the elements of an iterable to the end of the string
ljust()	Returns a left justified version of the string
lower()	Converts a string into lower case
lstrip()	Returns a left trim version of the string
maketrans()	Returns a translation table to be used in translations
partition()	Returns a tuple where the string is parted into three parts
replace()	Returns a string where a specified value is replaced with a specified value
rfind()	Searches the string for a specified value and returns the last position of where it was found
rindex()	Searches the string for a specified value and returns the last position of where it was found
rjust()	Returns a right justified version of the string
rpartition()	Returns a tuple where the string is parted into three parts
rsplit()	Splits the string at the specified separator, and returns a list
rstrip()	Returns a right trim version of the string
split()	Splits the string at the specified separator, and returns a list
splitlines()	Splits the string at line breaks and returns a list
startswith()	Returns true if the string starts with the specified value
strip()	Returns a trimmed version of the string
swapcase()	Swaps cases, lower case becomes upper case and vice versa
title()	Converts the first character of each word to upper case
translate()	Returns a translated string
upper()	Converts a string into upper case
zfill()	Fills the string with a specified number of 0 values at the beginning

Python Booleans

Booleans represent one of two values: `True` or `False`.

Section 8.1 - Boolean Values

In programming you often need to know if an expression is `True` or `False`.

You can evaluate any expression in Python, and get one of two answers, `True` or `False`.

When you compare two values, the expression is evaluated and Python returns the Boolean answer:

```
1  print(10 > 9)
2  print(10 == 9)
3  print(10 < 9)
```

When you run a condition in an if statement, Python returns `True` or `False`:

```
1  a = 150
2  b = 25
3
4  if b > a:
5    print("b is greater than a")
6  else:
7    print("b is not greater than a")
```

Section 8.2 - Evaluate Values and Variables

The `bool()` function allows you to evaluate any value, and give you `True` or `False` in return.

Evaluate a string and a number:

```
1  print(bool("Hello"))
2  print(bool(15))
```

Evaluate two variables:

```
1   x = "Hello"
2   y = 15
3
4   print(bool(x))
5   print(bool(y))
```

Section 8.3 - Most Values are True

Almost any value is evaluated to True if it has some sort of content.

Any string is True, except empty strings.

Any number is True, except 0.

Any list, tuple, set, and dictionary are True, except empty ones.

The following will return True:

```
1   bool("abc")
2   bool(123)
3   bool(["apple", "cherry", "banana"])
```

Section 8.4 - Some Values are False

In fact, there are not many values that evaluate to False, except empty values, such as (), [], {}, "",
the number 0, and the value None. And of course the value False evaluates to False.

The following will return False:

```
1   bool(False)
2   bool(None)
3   bool(0)
4   bool("")
5   bool(())
6   bool([])
7   bool({})
```

One more value, or object in this case, evaluates to False, and that is if you have an object that is
made from a class with a __len__ function that returns 0 or False:

```
1  class myclass():
2   def __len__(self):
3     return 0
4
5  myobj = myclass()
6  print(bool(myobj))
```

Section 8.5 - Functions can Return a Boolean

You can create functions that returns a Boolean Value:

Print the answer of a function:

```
1  def myFunction() :
2   return True
3
4  print(myFunction())
```

You can execute code based on the Boolean answer of a function:

Print "YES!" if the function returns True, otherwise print "NO!":

```
1  def myFunction() :
2   return True
3
4  if myFunction():
5   print("YES!")
6  else:
7   print("NO!")
```

Python also has many built-in functions that return a boolean value, like the isinstance() function, which can be used to determine if an object is of a certain data type:

Check if an object is an integer or not:

```
1  x = 200
2  print(isinstance(x, int))
```

Python Operators

Section 9.1 - Python Operators

Operators are used to perform operations on variables and values.

In the example below, we use the + operator to add together two values:

```
1  print(10 + 5)
```

Python divides the operators in the following groups:

- Arithmetic operators
- Assignment operators
- Comparison operators
- Logical operators
- Identity operators
- Membership operators
- Bitwise operators

Section 9.2 - Python Arithmetic Operators

Arithmetic operators are used with numeric values to perform common mathematical operations:

Operator	Name	Example
+	Addition	x + y
-	Subtraction	x - y
*	Multiplication	x * y
/	Division	x / y
%	Modulus	x % y
**	Exponentiation	x ** y
//	Floor division	x // y

Section 9.3 - Python Assignment Operators

Assignment operators are used to assign values to variables:

Operator	Example	Same As
=	x = 5	x = 5
+=	x += 3	x = x + 3
-=	x -= 3	x = x - 3
*=	x *= 3	x = x * 3
/=	x /= 3	x = x / 3
%=	x %= 3	x = x % 3
//=	x //= 3	x = x // 3
**=	x **= 3	x = x ** 3
&=	x &= 3	x = x & 3
`	=`	`x
^=	x ^= 3	x = x ^ 3
>>=	x >>= 3	x = x >> 3
<<=	x <<= 3	x = x << 3

Section 9.4 - Python Comparison Operators

Comparison operators are used to compare two values:

Operator	Name	Example
==	Equal	x == y
!=	Not equal	x != y
>	Greater than	x > y
<	Less than	x < y
>=	Greater than or equal to	x >= y
<=	Less than or equal to	x <= y

Section 9.5 - Python Logical Operators

Logical operators are used to combine conditional statements:

Operator	Description	Example
and	Returns True if both statements are true	x < 5 and x < 10
or	Returns True if one of the statements is true	x < 5 or x < 4
not	Reverse the result, returns False if the result is true	not(x < 5 and x < 10)

Section 9.6 - Python Identity Operators

Identity operators are used to compare the objects, not if they are equal, but if they are actually the same object, with the same memory location:

Operator	Description	Example
is	Returns True if both variables are the same object	x is y
is not	Returns True if both variables are not the same object	x is not y

Section 9.7 - Python Membership Operators

Membership operators are used to test if a sequence is presented in an object:

Operator	Description	Example
in	Returns True if a sequence with the specified value is present in the object	x in y
not in	Returns True if a sequence with the specified value is not present in the object	x not in y

Section 9.8 - Python Bitwise Operators

Bitwise operators are used to compare (binary) numbers:

Operator	Name	Description	Example
&	AND	Sets each bit to 1 if both bits are 1	x & y
|	OR	Sets each bit to 1 if one of two bits is 1	'x
^	XOR	Sets each bit to 1 if only one of two bits is 1	x ^ y
~	NOT	Inverts all the bits	~x
<<	Zero fill left shift	Shift left by pushing zeros in from the right and let the leftmost bits fall off	x << 2
>>	Signed right shift	Shift right by pushing copies of the leftmost bit in from the left, and let the rightmost bits fall off	x >> 2

Section 9.9 - Operator Precedence

Operator precedence describes the order in which operations are performed.

Parentheses has the highest precedence, meaning that expressions inside parentheses must be evaluated first:

```
1  print((6 + 3) - (6 + 3))
```

Multiplication * has higher precedence than addition +, and therefor multiplications are evaluated before additions:

```
1  print(100 + 5 * 3)
```

The precedence order is described in the table below, starting with the highest precedence at the top:

Operator	Description
( )	Parentheses
**	Exponentiation
+x -x ~x	Unary plus, unary minus, and bitwise NOT
* / // %	Multiplication, division, floor division, and modulus
+ -	Addition and subtraction
<< >>	Bitwise left and right shifts
&	Bitwise AND
^	Bitwise XOR
'	'

Operator	Description
== != > >= < <= is is not in not in	Comparisons, identity, and membership operators
not	Logical NOT
and	AND
or	OR

If two operators have the same precedence, the expression is evaluated from left to right.

Addition + and subtraction - has the same precedence, and therefor we evaluate the expression from left to right:

```
1  print(5 + 4 - 7 + 3)
```

Python Lists

Section 10.1 - List

Lists are used to store multiple items in a single variable.

Lists are one of 4 built-in data types in Python used to store collections of data, the other 3 are Tuple, Set, and Dictionary, all with different qualities and usage.

Lists are created using square brackets:

```
1  fruits = ["apple", "banana", "cherry"]
2  print(fruits)
```

Section 10.1.1 - List Items

List items are ordered, changeable, and allow duplicate values.

List items are indexed, the first item has index [0], the second item has index [1] etc.

Section 10.1.2 - Ordered

When we say that lists are ordered, it means that the items have a defined order, and that order will not change.

If you add new items to a list, the new items will be placed at the end of the list.

> **Note:** There are some list methods that will change the order, but in general: the order of the items will not change.

Section 10.1.3 - Changeable

The list is changeable, meaning that we can change, add, and remove items in a list after it has been created.

Section 10.1.4 - Allow Duplicates

Since lists are indexed, lists can have items with the same value:

```
1  fruits = ["apple", "banana", "cherry", "apple", "cherry"]
2  print(fruits)
```

Section 10.1.5 - List Length

To determine how many items a list has, use the `len()` function:

```
1  fruits = ["apple", "banana", "cherry"]
2  print(len(fruits))
```

Section 10.2 - List Items - Data Types

List items can be of any data type:

```
1  string_list = ["apple", "banana", "cherry"]
2  integer_list = [1, 5, 7, 9, 3]
3  boolean_list = [True, False, False]
```

A list can contain different data types.

A list with strings, integers and boolean values:

```
1  mixed_list = ["abc", 34, True, 40, "male"]
```

Section 10.2.1 - `type()`

From Python's perspective, lists are defined as objects with the data type 'list':

```
1  <class 'list'>
```

What is the data type of a list?

```
1  fruits = ["apple", "banana", "cherry"]
2  print(type(fruits)) # prints <class 'list'>
```

Section 10.2.2 - The list() Constructor

It is also possible to use the list() constructor when creating a new list.

Using the `list()` constructor to make a List:

```
1  fruits = list(("apple", "banana", "cherry")) # note the double round-brackets
2  print(fruits)
```

Section 10.3 - Access List Items

Section 10.3.1 - Access Items

List items are indexed and you can access them by referring to the index number.

Print the second item of the list:

```
1  fruits = ["apple", "banana", "cherry"]
2  print(fruits[1])
```

Note: The first item has index 0.

Section 10.3.2 - Negative Indexing

Negative indexing means start from the end

-1 refers to the last item, -2 refers to the second last item etc.

Print the last item of the list:

```
1  fruits = ["apple", "banana", "cherry"]
2  print(fruits[-1])
```

Section 10.3.3 - Range of Indexes

You can specify a range of indexes by specifying where to start and where to end the range.

When specifying a range, the return value will be a new list with the specified items.

```
1  fruits = ["apple", "banana", "cherry", "orange", "kiwi", "melon", "mango"]
2  print(fruits[2:5])
```

Note: The search will start at index 2 (included) and end at index 5 (not included).

Remember that the first item has index 0.

This example returns the items from the beginning to, but NOT including, "kiwi":

```
1  fruits = ["apple", "banana", "cherry", "orange", "kiwi", "melon", "mango"]
2  print(fruits[:4])
```

By leaving out the end value, the range will go on to the end of the list.

This example returns the items from "cherry" to the end:

```
1  fruits = ["apple", "banana", "cherry", "orange", "kiwi", "melon", "mango"]
2  print(fruits[2:])
```

Section 10.3.4 - Range of Negative Indexes

Specify negative indexes if you want to start the search from the end of the list.

This example returns the items from "orange" (-4) to, but NOT including "mango" (-1):

```
1  fruits = ["apple", "banana", "cherry", "orange", "kiwi", "melon", "mango"]
2  print(fruits[-4:-1])
```

Section 10.3.5 - Check if Item Exists

To determine if a specified item is present in a list use the in keyword.

Check if "apple" is present in the list:

```
1  fruits = ["apple", "banana", "cherry"]
2  if "apple" in fruits:
3   print("Yes, 'apple' is in the fruits list")
```

Section 10.4 - Change List Items

Section 10.4.1 - Change Item Value

To change the value of a specific item, refer to the index number.

Change the second item:

```
1  fruits = ["apple", "banana", "cherry"]
2  fruits[1] = "blackberry"
3  print(fruits)
```

Section 10.4.2 - Change a Range of Item Values

To change the value of items within a specific range, define a list with the new values, and refer to the range of index numbers where you want to insert the new values.

Change the values "banana" and "cherry" with the values "blackberry" and "watermelon":

```
1  fruits = ["apple", "banana", "cherry", "orange", "kiwi", "mango"]
2  fruits[1:3] = ["blackberry", "watermelon"]
3  print(fruits)
```

If you insert *more* items than you replace, the new items will be inserted where you specified, and the remaining items will move accordingly.

Change the second value by replacing it with *two* new values:

```
1  fruits = ["apple", "banana", "cherry"]
2  fruits[1:2] = ["blackcurrant", "watermelon"]
3  print(fruits)
```

> **Note:** The length of the list will change when the number of items inserted does not match the number of items replaced.

If you insert *less* items than you replace, the new items will be inserted where you specified, and the remaining items will move accordingly.

Change the second and third value by replacing it with *one* value:

```
1  fruits = ["apple", "banana", "cherry"]
2  fruits[1:3] = ["watermelon"]
3  print(fruits)
```

Section 10.4.3 - Insert Items

To insert a new list item, without replacing any of the existing values, we can use the insert() method.

The insert() method inserts an item at the specified index.

Insert "watermelon" as the third item:

```
1  fruits = ["apple", "banana", "cherry"]
2  fruits.insert(2, "watermelon")
3  print(fruits)
```

Note: As a result of the example above, the list will now contain 4 items.

Section 10.5 - Add List Items

Section 10.5.1 - Append Items

To add an item to the end of the list, use the append() method.

Using the append() method to append an item:

```
1  fruits = ["apple", "banana", "cherry"]
2  fruits.append("orange")
3  print(fruits)
```

Section 10.5.2 - Insert Items

To insert a list item at a specified index, use the insert() method.

The insert() method inserts an item at the specified index.

Insert an item as the second position:

```
1  fruits = ["apple", "banana", "cherry"]
2  fruits.insert(1, "orange")
3  print(fruits)
```

Note: As a result of the examples above, the lists will now contain 4 items.

Section 10.5.3 - Extend List

To append elements from *another list* to the current list, use the extend() method.

Add the elements of tropical to fruits:

```
1   fruits = ["apple", "banana", "cherry"]
2   tropical_fruits = ["mango", "pineapple", "papaya"]
3   fruits.extend(tropical_fruits)
4   print(fruits)
```

The elements will be added to the *end* of the list.

Section 10.5.4 - Add Any Iterable

The extend() method does not have to append *lists*, you can add any iterable object (tuples, sets, dictionaries etc.).

Add elements of a tuple to a list:

```
1   fruits = ["apple", "banana", "cherry"]
2   fruits_tuple = ("kiwi", "orange")
3   fruits.extend(fruits_tuple)
4   print(fruits)
```

Section 10.6 - Remove List Items

Section 10.6.1 - Remove Specified Item

The remove() method removes the specified item.

Remove "banana":

```
1   fruits = ["apple", "banana", "cherry"]
2   fruits.remove("banana")
3   print(fruits)
```

If there are more than one item with the specified value, the remove() method removes the first occurrence.

Remove the first occurrence of "banana":

```
1   fruits = ["apple", "banana", "cherry", "banana", "kiwi"]
2   fruits.remove("banana")
3   print(fruits)
```

Section 10.6.2 - Remove Specified Index

The pop() method removes the specified index.

Remove the second item:

```
1   fruits = ["apple", "banana", "cherry"]
2   fruits.pop(1)
3   print(fruits)
```

If you do not specify the index, the pop() method removes the last item.

Remove the last item:

```
1   fruits = ["apple", "banana", "cherry"]
2   fruits.pop()
3   print(fruits)
```

The del keyword also removes the specified index.

Remove the first item:

```
1   fruits = ["apple", "banana", "cherry"]
2   del fruits[0]
3   print(fruits)
```

The del keyword can also delete the list completely.

Delete the entire list:

```
1   fruits = ["apple", "banana", "cherry"]
2   del fruits
```

Section 10.6.3 - Clear the List

The clear() method empties the list.

The list still remains, but it has no content.

Clear the list content:

```
1   fruits = ["apple", "banana", "cherry"]
2   fruits.clear()
3   print(fruits)
```

Section 10.7 - Loop Lists

Section 10.7.1 - Loop Through a List

You can loop through the list items by using a for loop:

Print all items in the list, one by one:

```
1  fruits = ["apple", "banana", "cherry"]
2  for x in fruits:
3    print(x)
```

Section 10.7.2 - Loop Through the Index Numbers

You can also loop through the list items by referring to their index number.

Use the range() and len() functions to create a suitable iterable.

Print all items by referring to their index number:

```
1  fruits = ["apple", "banana", "cherry"]
2  for i in range(len(fruits)):
3    print(fruits[i])
```

The iterable created in the example above is [0, 1, 2].

Section 10.7.3 - Using a While Loop

You can loop through the list items by using a while loop.

Use the len() function to determine the length of the list, then start at 0 and loop your way through the list items by referring to their indexes.

Remember to increase the index by 1 after each iteration.

Print all items, using a while loop to go through all the index numbers:

```
1  fruits = ["apple", "banana", "cherry"]
2  i = 0
3  while i < len(fruits):
4    print(fruits[i])
5    i = i + 1
```

Section 10.7.4 - Looping Using List Comprehension

List Comprehension offers the shortest syntax for looping through lists

A short hand for loop that will print all items in a list:

```
1  fruits = ["apple", "banana", "cherry"]
2  [print(x) for x in fruits]
```

Section 10.8 - List Comprehension

Section 10.8.1 - List Comprehension

List comprehension offers a shorter syntax when you want to create a new list based on the values of an existing list.

Example:

Based on a list of fruits, you want a new list, containing only the fruits with the letter "a" in the name.

Without list comprehension you will have to write a for statement with a conditional test inside:

```
1  fruits = ["apple", "banana", "cherry", "kiwi", "mango"]
2  new_fruits_list = []
3
4  for x in fruits:
5   if "a" in x:
6     new_fruits_list.append(x)
7
8  print(new_fruits_list)
```

With list comprehension you can do all that with only one line of code:

```
1  fruits = ["apple", "banana", "cherry", "kiwi", "mango"]
2
3  new_fruits_list = [x for x in fruits if "a" in x]
4
5  print(new_fruits_list)
```

Section 10.8.2 - The Syntax

```
1    newlist = [expression for item in iterable if condition == True]
```

The return value is a new list, leaving the old list unchanged.

Section 10.8.2.1 - Condition

The *condition* is like a filter that only accepts the items that valuate to `True`.

Example:
Only accept items that are not `"apple"`:

```
1    new_fruits_list = [x for x in fruits if x != "apple"]
```

The condition `if x != "apple"` will return `True` for all elements other than `"apple"`, making the new fruits list contain all fruits except `"apple"`.

The *condition* is optional and can be omitted.

Example:
With no `if` statement:

```
1    new_fruits_list = [x for x in fruits]
```

Section 10.8.2.2 - Iterable

The *iterable* can be any iterable object, like a list, tuple, set etc.

Example:
You can use the `range()` function to create an iterable:

```
1    new_fruits_list = [x for x in range(10)]
```

Same example, but with a condition:

Example:
Accept only numbers lower than 5:

```
1  new_fruits_list = [x for x in range(10) if x < 5]
```

Section 10.8.2.3 - Expression

The *expression* is the current item in the iteration, but it is also the outcome, which you can manipulate before it ends up like a list item in the new fruits list:

Example:
Set the values in the new fruits list to upper case:

```
1  new_fruits_list = [x.upper() for x in fruits]
```

You can set the outcome to whatever you like.

Example:
Set all values in the new fruits list to `'hello'`:

```
1  new_fruits_list = ['hello' for x in fruits]
```

The *expression* can also contain conditions, not like a filter, but as a way to manipulate the outcome.

Example:
Return "orange" instead of "banana":

```
1  new_fruits_list = [x if x != "banana" else "orange" for x in fruits]
```

The *expression* in the example above says:

"Return the item if it is not banana, if it is banana return orange".

Section 10.9 - Sort Lists

Section 10.9.1 - Sort List Alphanumerically

List objects have a `sort()` method that will sort the list alphanumerically, ascending, by default:

Example:
Sort the list alphabetically:

```
1  fruits = ["orange", "mango", "kiwi", "pineapple", "banana"]
2  fruits.sort()
3  print(fruits)
```

Example:

Sort the list numerically:

```
1  numbers_list = [100, 50, 65, 82, 23]
2  numbers_list.sort()
3  print(numbers_list)
```

Section 10.9.2 - Sort Descending

To sort descending, use the keyword argument `reverse = True`:

Example:

Sort the list descending:

```
1  fruits = ["orange", "mango", "kiwi", "pineapple", "banana"]
2  fruits.sort(reverse = True)
3  print(fruits)
```

Example:

Sort the list descending:

```
1  numbers_list = [100, 50, 65, 82, 23]
2  numbers_list.sort(reverse = True)
3  print(numbers_list)
```

Section 10.9.3 - Customize Sort Function

You can also customize your own function by using the keyword argument `key = *function*`.

The function will return a number that will be used to sort the list (the lowest number first):

Example:

Sort the list based on how close the number is to 50:

```
1  def myfunc(n):
2    return abs(n - 50)
3
4  numbers_list = [100, 50, 65, 82, 23]
5  numbers_list.sort(key = myfunc)
6  print(numbers_list)
```

Section 10.9.4 - Case Insensitive Sort

By default the sort() method is case sensitive, resulting in all capital letters being sorted before lower case letters:

Example:

Case sensitive sorting can give an unexpected result:

```
1  fruits = ["banana", "Orange", "Kiwi", "cherry"]
2  fruits.sort()
3  print(fruits)
```

Luckily we can use built-in functions as key functions when sorting a list.

So if you want a case-insensitive sort function, use str.lower as a key function:

Example:

Perform a case-insensitive sort of the list:

```
1  fruits = ["banana", "Orange", "Kiwi", "cherry"]
2  fruits.sort(key = str.lower)
3  print(fruits)
```

Section 10.9.5 - Reverse Order

What if you want to reverse the order of a list, regardless of the alphabet?

The reverse() method reverses the current sorting order of the elements.

Example:

Reverse the order of the list items:

```
1  fruits = ["banana", "Orange", "Kiwi", "cherry"]
2  fruits.reverse()
3  print(fruits)
```

Section 10.10 - Copy Lists

Section 10.10.1 - Copy a List

You cannot copy a list simply by typing list2 = list1, because: list2 will only be a *reference* to list1, and changes made in list1 will automatically also be made in list2.

There are ways to make a copy, one way is to use the built-in List method copy().

> **Example:**
>
> Make a copy of a list with the copy() method:

```
1  fruits = ["apple", "banana", "cherry"]
2  new_fruits_list = fruits.copy()
3  print(new_fruits_list)
```

Another way to make a copy is to use the built-in method list().

> **Example:**
>
> Make a copy of a list with the list() method:

```
1  fruits = ["apple", "banana", "cherry"]
2  new_fruits_list = list(fruits)
3  print(new_fruits_list)
```

Section 10.11 - Join Lists

Section 10.11.1 - Join Two Lists

There are several ways to join, or concatenate, two or more lists in Python.

One of the easiest ways are by using the + operator.

> **Example:**
>
> Join two list:

```
1  char_list = ["a", "b", "c"]
2  int_list = [1, 2, 3]
3
4  combine_list = char_list + int_list
5  print(combine_list)
```

Another way to join two lists is by appending all the items from int_list into char_list, one by one:

Example:

Append int_list into char_list:

```
1  char_list = ["a", "b" , "c"]
2  int_list = [1, 2, 3]
3
4  for x in int_list:
5   char_list.append(x)
6
7  print(char_list)
```

Or you can use the extend() method, where the purpose is to add elements from one list to another list:

Example:

Use the extend() method to add int_list at the end of char_list:

```
1  char_list = ["a", "b" , "c"]
2  int_list = [1, 2, 3]
3
4  char_list.extend(int_list)
5  print(char_list)
```

Section 10.12 - List Methods

Section 10.12.1 - List Methods

Python has a set of built-in methods that you can use on lists.

Method	Description
append()	Adds an element at the end of the list
clear()	Removes all the elements from the list
copy()	Returns a copy of the list
count()	Returns the number of elements with the specified value
extend()	Add the elements of a list (or any iterable), to the end of the current list
index()	Returns the index of the first element with the specified value
insert()	Adds an element at the specified position
pop()	Removes the element at the specified position
remove()	Removes the item with the specified value
reverse()	Reverses the order of the list
sort()	Sorts the list

Python Tuples

Section 11.1 - Tuple

Tuples are used to store multiple items in a single variable.

Tuple is one of 4 built-in data types in Python used to store collections of data, the other 3 are List[1], Set[2], and Dictionary[3], all with different qualities and usage.

A tuple is a collection which is ordered and **unchangeable**.

Tuples are written with round brackets.

> **Example:**
>
> Create a tuple

```
1  fruits_tuple = ("apple", "banana", "cherry")
```

Section 11.1.1 - Tuple Items

Tuple items are ordered, unchangeable, and allow duplicate values.

Tuple items are indexed, the first item has index [0], the second item has index [1] etc.

Section 11.1.2 - Ordered

When we say that tuples are ordered, it means that the items have a defined order, and that order will not change.

Section 11.1.3 - Unchangeable

Tuples are unchangeable, meaning that we cannot change, add or remove items after the tuple has been created.

---

[1]https://www.w3schools.com/python/python_lists.asp
[2]https://www.w3schools.com/python/python_sets.asp
[3]https://www.w3schools.com/python/python_dictionaries.asp

Section 11.1.4 - Allow Duplicates

Since tuples are indexed, they can have items with the same value:

Example:

Tuples allow duplicate values:

```
1  fruits_tuple = ("apple", "banana", "cherry", "apple", "cherry")
2  print(fruits_tuple)
```

Section 11.1.5 - Tuple Length

To determine how many items a tuple has, use the `len()` function:

Example:

Print the number of items in the tuple:

```
1  fruits_tuple = ("apple", "banana", "cherry")
2  print(len(fruits_tuple))
```

Section 11.1.6 - Create Tuple With One Item

To create a tuple with only one item, you have to add a comma after the item, otherwise Python will not recognize it as a tuple.

Example:

One item tuple, remember the comma:

```
1  fruits_tuple = ("apple",)
2  print(type(fruits_tuple))
3
4  #NOT a tuple
5  fruits_tuple = ("apple")
6  print(type(fruits_tuple))
```

Section 11.1.7 - Tuple Items - Data Types

Tuple items can be of any data type:

Example:

String, int and boolean data types:

```
1  fruits_tuple = ("apple", "banana", "cherry")
2  integer_tuple = (1, 5, 7, 9, 3)
3  boolean_tuple = (True, False, False)
```

A tuple can contain different data types:

Example:

A tuple with strings, integers and boolean values:

```
1  mixed_tuple = ("abc", 34, True, 40, "male")
```

Section 11.1.8 - `type()`

From Python's perspective, tuples are defined as objects with the data type 'tuple':

```
1  <class 'tuple'>
```

Example:

What is the data type of a tuple?

```
1  fruits_tuple = ("apple", "banana", "cherry")
2  print(type(fruits_tuple))
```

Section 11.1.9 - The `tuple()` Constructor

It is also possible to use the `tuple()` constructor to make a tuple.

Example:

Using the `tuple()` method to make a tuple:

```
1  fruits_tuple = tuple(("apple", "banana", "cherry")) # note the double round-brackets
2  print(fruits_tuple)
```

Section 11.2 - Access Tuple Items

Section 11.2.1 - Access Tuple Items

You can access tuple items by referring to the index number, inside square brackets:

Example:

Print the second item in the tuple:

```
1  fruits_tuple = ("apple", "banana", "cherry")
2  print(fruits_tuple[1])
```

> **Note:** The first item has index 0.

Section 11.2.2 - Negative Indexing

Negative indexing means start from the end.

-1 refers to the last item, -2 refers to the second last item etc.

> **Example:**
> Print the last item of the tuple:

```
1  fruits_tuple = ("apple", "banana", "cherry")
2  print(fruits_tuple[-1])
```

Section 11.2.3 - Range of Indexes

You can specify a range of indexes by specifying where to start and where to end the range.

When specifying a range, the return value will be a new tuple with the specified items.

> **Example:**
> Return the third, fourth, and fifth item:

```
1  fruits_tuple = ("apple", "banana", "cherry", "orange", "kiwi", "melon", "mango")
2  print(fruits_tuple[2:5])
```

> **Note:** The search will start at index 2 (included) and end at index 5 (not included).

Remember that the first item has index 0.

By leaving out the start value, the range will start at the first item:

> **Example:**
> This example returns the items from the beginning to, but NOT included, "kiwi":

```
1  fruits_tuple = ("apple", "banana", "cherry", "orange", "kiwi", "melon", "mango")
2  print(fruits_tuple[:4])
```

By leaving out the end value, the range will go on to the end of the list:

Example:

This example returns the items from "cherry" and to the end:

```
1  fruits_tuple = ("apple", "banana", "cherry", "orange", "kiwi", "melon", "mango")
2  print(fruits_tuple[2:])
```

Section 11.2.4 - Range of Negative Indexes

Specify negative indexes if you want to start the search from the end of the tuple:

Example:

This example returns the items from index -4 (included) to index -1 (excluded)

```
1  fruits_tuple = ("apple", "banana", "cherry", "orange", "kiwi", "melon", "mango")
2  print(fruits_tuple[-4:-1])
```

Section 11.2.5 - Check if Item Exists

To determine if a specified item is present in a tuple use the in keyword:

Example:

Check if "apple" is present in the tuple:

```
1  fruits_tuple = ("apple", "banana", "cherry")
2  if "apple" in fruits_tuple:
3   print("Yes, 'apple' is in the fruits tuple")
```

Section 11.3 - Update Tuples

Tuples are unchangeable, meaning that you cannot change, add, or remove items once the tuple is created.

But there are some workarounds.

Section 11.3.1 - Change Tuple Values

Once a tuple is created, you cannot change its values. Tuples are **unchangeable**, or **immutable** as it also is called.

But there is a workaround. You can convert the tuple into a list, change the list, and convert the list back into a tuple.

Example:

Convert the tuple into a list to be able to change it:

```
1  a = ("apple", "banana", "cherry")
2  b = list(a)
3  b[1] = "kiwi"
4  a = tuple(b)
5
6  print(a)
```

Section 11.3.2 - Add Items

Since tuples are immutable, they do not have a built-in append() method, but there are other ways to add items to a tuple.

1. **Convert into a list**: Just like the workaround for *changing* a tuple, you can convert it into a list, add your item(s), and convert it back into a tuple.

   Example:

   Convert the tuple into a list, add "orange", and convert it back into a tuple:

```
1  fruits_tuple = ("apple", "banana", "cherry")
2  fruits_list = list(fruits_tuple)
3  fruits_list.append("orange")
4  fruits_tuple = tuple(fruits_list)
5  print(fruits_list)
```

2. **Add tuple to a tuple.** You are allowed to add tuples to tuples, so if you want to add one item, (or many), create a new tuple with the item(s), and add it to the existing tuple:

   Example:

   Create a new tuple with the value "orange", and add that tuple:

```
1  fruits_tuple = ("apple", "banana", "cherry")
2  new_fruits_tuple = ("orange",)
3  fruits_tuple += new_fruits_tuple
4
5  print(fruits_tuple)
```

Note: When creating a tuple with only one item, remember to include a comma after the item, otherwise it will not be identified as a tuple.

Section 11.3.3 - Remove Items

Note: You cannot remove items in a tuple.

Tuples are **unchangeable**, so you cannot remove items from it, but you can use the same workaround as we used for changing and adding tuple items:

Example:

Convert the tuple into a list, remove "apple", and convert it back into a tuple:

```
1  fruits_tuple = ("apple", "banana", "cherry")
2  fruits_list = list(fruits_tuple)
3  fruits_list.remove("apple")
4  fruits_tuple = tuple(fruits_list)
5  print(fruits_tuple)
```

Or you can delete the tuple completely:

Example:

The del keyword can delete the tuple completely:

```
1  fruits_tuple = ("apple", "banana", "cherry")
2  del fruits_tuple
3  print(fruits_tuple) #this will raise an error because the tuple no longer exists
```

Section 11.4 - Unpack Tuples

Section 11.4.1 - Unpacking a Tuple

When we create a tuple, we normally assign values to it. This is called "packing" a tuple:

Example:

Packing a tuple:

```
1  fruits_tuple = ("apple", "banana", "cherry")
2
3  (green, yellow, red) = fruits_tuple
4
5  print(green)
6  print(yellow)
7  print(red)
```

Note: The number of variables must match the number of values in the tuple, if not, you must use an asterisk to collect the remaining values as a list.

Section 11.4.2 - Using Asterisk*

If the number of variables is less than the number of values, you can add an * to the variable name and the values will be assigned to the variable as a list:

Example:

Assign the rest of the values as a list called "red":

```
1  fruits_tuple = ("apple", "banana", "cherry", "strawberry", "raspberry")
2
3  (green, yellow, *red) = fruits_tuple
4
5  print(green)
6  print(yellow)
7  print(red)
```

If the asterisk is added to another variable name than the last, Python will assign values to the variable until the number of values left matches the number of variables left.

Example:

Add a list of values the "tropic" variable:

```
1   fruits_tuple = ("apple", "mango", "papaya", "pineapple", "cherry")
2
3   (green, *tropic, red) = fruits_tuple
4
5   print(green)
6   print(tropic)
7   print(red)
```

Section 11.5 - Loop Tuples

Section 11.5.1 - Loop Through a Tuple

You can loop through the tuple items by using a for loop.

> **Example:**
> Iterate through the items and print the values:

```
1   fruits_tuple = ("apple", "banana", "cherry")
2   for fruit in fruits_tuple:
3    print(fruit)
```

Section 11.5.2 - Loop Through the Index Numbers

You can also loop through the tuple items by referring to their index number.

Use the range() and len() functions to create a suitable iterable.

> **Example:**
> Print all items by referring to their index number:

```
1   fruits_tuple = ("apple", "banana", "cherry")
2   for i in range(len(fruits_tuple)):
3    print(fruits_tuple[i])
```

Section 11.5.3 - Using a While Loop

You can loop through the tuple items by using a `while` loop.

Use the `len()` function to determine the length of the tuple, then start at 0 and loop your way through the tuple items by referring to their indexes.

Remember to increase the index by 1 after each iteration.

Example:

Print all items, using a `while` loop to go through all the index numbers:

```
1  fruits_tuple = ("apple", "banana", "cherry")
2  i = 0
3  while i < len(fruits_tuple):
4   print(fruits_tuple[i])
5    i = i + 1
```

Section 11.6 - Join Tuples

Section 11.6.1 - Join Two Tuples

To join two or more tuples you can use the + operator:

Example:
Join two tuples:

```
1  char_tuple = ("a", "b" , "c")
2  int_tuple = (1, 2, 3)
3
4  combine_tuple = char_tuple + int_tuple
5  print(combine_tuple)
```

Section 11.6.2 - Multiply Tuples

If you want to multiply the content of a tuple a given number of times, you can use the * operator:

Example:
Multiply the fruits tuple by 2:

```
1  fruits_tuple = ("apple", "banana", "cherry")
2  combined_tuples = fruits_tuple * 2
3
4  print(combined_tuples)
```

Section 11.7 - Tuple Methods

Section 11.7.1 - Tuple Methods

Python has two built-in methods that you can use on tuples.

Method	Description
count()[4]	Returns the number of times a specified value occurs in a tuple
index()[5]	Searches the tuple for a specified value and returns the position of where it was found

Python Sets

Section 12.1 - Set

Sets are used to store multiple items in a single variable.

Set is one of 4 built-in data types in Python used to store collections of data, the other 3 are List, Tuple, and Dictionary, all with different qualities and usage.

A set is a collection which is *unordered, unchangeable*[^^* **Note:** Set *items* are unchangeable, but you can remove items and add new items.], and *unindexed.*

Sets are written with curly brackets.

> **Example:**
> Create a Set:

```
1  fruits_set = {"apple", "banana", "cherry"}
2  print(fruits_set)
```

Section 12.1.1 - Set Items

Set items are unordered, unchangeable, and do not allow duplicate values.

Section 12.1.2 - Unordered

Unordered means that the items in a set do not have a defined order.

Set items can appear in a different order every time you use them, and cannot be referred to by index or key.

Section 12.1.3 - Unchangeable

Set items are unchangeable, meaning that we cannot change the items after the set has been created.

Once a set is created, you cannot change its items, but you can remove items and add new items.

Section 12.1.4 - Duplicates Not Allowed

Sets cannot have two items with the same value.

Example:

Duplicate values will be ignored:

```
1  fruits_set = {"apple", "banana", "cherry", "apple"}
2
3  print(fruits_set)
```

Note: The values `True` and `1` are considered the same value in sets, and are treated as duplicates:

Example:

True and 1 is considered the same value:

```
1  fruits_set = {"apple", "banana", "cherry", True, 1, 2}
2
3  print(fruits_set)
```

Section 12.1.5 - Get the Length of a Set

To determine how many items a set has, use the `len()` function.

Example:

Get the number of items in a set:

```
1  fruits_set = {"apple", "banana", "cherry"}
2
3  print(len(fruits_set))
```

Section 12.1.6 - Set Items - Data Types

Set items can be of any data type:

Example:

String, int and boolean data types:

```
1  string_set = {"apple", "banana", "cherry"}
2  integer_set = {1, 5, 7, 9, 3}
3  boolean_set = {True, False, False}
```

A set can contain different data types:

Example:
A set with strings, integers and boolean values:

```
1  mixed_type_set = {"abc", 34, True, 40, "male"}
```

Section 12.1.7 - `type()`

From Python's perspective, sets are defined as objects with the data type `'set'`:

```
1  <class 'set'>
```

Example:
What is the data type of a set?

```
1  fruits_set = {"apple", "banana", "cherry"}
2  print(type(fruits_set))
```

Section 12.1.8 - The `set()` Constructor

It is also possible to use the `set()` constructor to make a set.

Example:
Using the `set()` constructor to make a set:

```
1  fruits_set = set(("apple", "banana", "cherry")) # note the double round-brackets
2  print(fruits_set)
```

Section 12.2 - Access Set Items

Section - 12.2.1 - Access Items

You cannot access items in a set by referring to an index or a key.

But you can loop through the set items using a for loop, or ask if a specified value is present in a set, by using the in keyword.

Example:

Loop through the set, and print the values:

```
1  fruits_set = {"apple", "banana", "cherry"}
2
3  for fruit in fruits_set:
4   print(fruit)
```

Example:

Check if "banana" is present in the set:

```
1  fruits_set = {"apple", "banana", "cherry"}
2
3  print("banana" in fruits_set)
```

Section 12.3 - Add Set Items

Section 12.3.1 - Add Items

Once a set is created, you cannot change its items, but you can add new items.

To add one item to a set use the add() method.

Example:

Add an item to a set, using the add() method:

```
1   fruits_set = {"apple", "banana", "cherry"}
2
3   fruits_set.add("orange")
4
5   print(fruits_set)
```

Section 12.3.2 - Add Sets

To add items from another set into the current set, use the update() method.

Example:

Add elements from tropical into fruits_set:

```
1   fruits_set = {"apple", "banana", "cherry"}
2   tropical = {"pineapple", "mango", "papaya"}
3
4   fruits_set.update(tropical)
5
6   print(fruits_set)
```

Section 12.3.3 - Add Any Iterable

The object in the update() method does not have to be a set, it can be any iterable object (tuples, lists, dictionaries etc.).

Example:

Add elements of a list to at set:

```
1   fruits_set = {"apple", "banana", "cherry"}
2   fruits_list = ["kiwi", "orange"]
3
4   fruits_set.update(fruits_list)
5
6   print(fruits_set)
```

Section 12.4 - Remove Set Items

Section 12.4.1 - Remove Item

To remove an item in a set, use the `remove()`, or the `discard()` method.

Example:
Remove "banana" by using the `remove()` method:

```
1   fruits_set = {"apple", "banana", "cherry"}
2
3   fruits_set.remove("banana")
4
5   print(fruits_set)
```

Note: If the item to remove does not exist, `remove()` will raise an error.

Example:
Remove "banana" by using the `discard()` method:

```
1   fruits_set = {"apple", "banana", "cherry"}
2
3   fruits_set.discard("banana")
4
5   print(fruits_set)
```

Note: If the item to remove does not exist, `discard()` will **NOT** raise an error.

You can also use the `pop()` method to remove an item, but this method will remove a random item, so you cannot be sure what item that gets removed.

The return value of the `pop()` method is the removed item.

Example:
Remove a random item by using the `pop()` method:

```
1   fruits_set = {"apple", "banana", "cherry"}
2
3   x = fruits_set.pop()
4
5   print(x)
6
7   print(fruits_set)
```

Note: Sets are *unordered*, so when using the pop() method, you do not know which item that gets removed.

Example:

The clear() method empties the set:

```
1   fruits_set = {"apple", "banana", "cherry"}
2
3   fruits_set.clear()
4
5   print(fruits_set)
```

Example:

The del keyword will delete the set completely:

```
1   fruits_set = {"apple", "banana", "cherry"}
2
3   del fruits_set
4
5   print(fruits_set)
```

Section 12.5 - Loop Sets

Section 12.5.1 - Loop Items

You can loop through the set items by using a for loop:

Example:

Loop through the set, and print the values:

```
1  fruits_set = {"apple", "banana", "cherry"}
2
3  for x in fruits_set:
4   print(x)
```

Section 12.6 - Join Sets

Section 12.6.1 - Join Two Sets

There are several ways to join two or more sets in Python.

You can use the union() method that returns a new set containing all items from both sets, or the update() method that inserts all the items from one set into another:

Example:

The union() method returns a new set with all items from both sets:

```
1  char_set = {"a", "b" , "c"}
2  integer_set = {1, 2, 3}
3
4  combine_set = char_set.union(integer_set)
5  print(combine_set)
```

Example:

The update() method inserts the items in integer_set into char_set:

```
1  char_set = {"a", "b" , "c"}
2  integer_set = {1, 2, 3}
3
4  combine_set.update(integer_set)
5  print(combine_set)
```

Note: Both union() and update() will exclude any duplicate items.

Section 12.6.2 - Keep ONLY the Duplicates

The intersection_update() method will keep only the items that are present in both sets.

Example:

Keep the items that exist in both set x, and set y:

```
1  x = {"apple", "banana", "cherry"}
2  y = {"google", "microsoft", "apple"}
3
4  x.intersection_update(y)
5
6  print(x)
```

The intersection() method will return a *new* set, that only contains the items that are present in both sets.

Example:
Return a set that contains the items that exist in both set x, and set y:

```
1  x = {"apple", "banana", "cherry"}
2  y = {"kiwi", "pineapple", "apple"}
3
4  z = x.intersection(y)
5
6  print(z)
```

Section 12.6.3 - Keep All, But NOT the Duplicates

The symmetric_difference_update() method will keep only the elements that are NOT present in both sets.

Example:
Keep the items that are not present in both sets:

```
1  x = {"apple", "banana", "cherry"}
2  y = {"kiwi", "pineapple", "apple"}
3
4  x.symmetric_difference_update(y)
5
6  print(x)
```

The symmetric_difference() method will return a new set, that contains only the elements that are NOT present in both sets.

Example:
Return a set that contains all items from both sets, except items that are present in both:

```
1  x = {"apple", "banana", "cherry"}
2  y = {"kiwi", "pineapple", "apple"}
3
4  z = x.symmetric_difference(y)
5
6  print(z)
```

Note: The values True and 1 are considered the same value in sets, and are treated as duplicates:

   Example:

   True and 1 is considered the same value:

```
1  x = {"apple", "banana", "cherry", True}
2  y = {"kiwi", 1, "apple", 2}
3
4  z = x.symmetric_difference(y)
5
6  print(z)
```

Section 12.7 - Set Methods

Section 12.7.1 - Set Methods

Python has a set of built-in methods that you can use on sets.

Method	Description
add()	Adds an element to the set
clear()	Removes all the elements from the set
copy()	Returns a copy of the set
difference()	Returns a set containing the difference between two or more sets
difference_update()	Removes the items in this set that are also included in another, specified set
discard()	Remove the specified item
intersection()	Returns a set, that is the intersection of two other sets
intersection_update()	Removes the items in this set that are not present in other, specified set(s)

Method	Description
`isdisjoint()`	Returns whether two sets have a intersection or not
`issubset()`	Returns whether another set contains this set or not
`issuperset()`	Returns whether this set contains another set or not
`pop()`	Removes an element from the set
`remove()`	Removes the specified element
`symmetric_difference()`	Returns a set with the symmetric differences of two sets
`symmetric_difference_update()`	inserts the symmetric differences from this set and another
`union()`	Return a set containing the union of sets
`update()`	Update the set with the union of this set and others

Python Dictionaries

Section 13.1 - Dictionary

Dictionaries are used to store data values in key:value pairs.

A dictionary is a collection which is ordered*, changeable and do not allow duplicates.

As of Python version 3.7, dictionaries are *ordered*. In Python 3.6 and earlier, dictionaries are *unordered*.

Dictionaries are written with curly brackets, and have keys and values:

Example:

Create and print a dictionary:

```
1  car_dict = {
2    "brand": "Acura",
3    "model": "MDX",
4    "year": 2023
5  }
6  print(car_dict)
```

Section 13.1.1 - Dictionary Items

Dictionary items are ordered, changeable, and does not allow duplicates.

Dictionary items are presented in key:value pairs, and can be referred to by using the key name.

Example:

Print the "brand" value of the dictionary:

```
1  car_dict =  {
2   "brand": "Acura",
3   "model": "MDX",
4   "year": 2023
5  }
6  print(car_dict["brand"])
```

Section 13.1.2 - Ordered or Unordered?

As of Python version 3.7, dictionaries are *ordered*. In Python 3.6 and earlier, dictionaries are *unordered.*

When we say that dictionaries are ordered, it means that the items have a defined order, and that order will not change.

Unordered means that the items does not have a defined order, you cannot refer to an item by using an index.

*   *   *

Section 13.1.3 - Changeable

Dictionaries are changeable, meaning that we can change, add or remove items after the dictionary has been created.

*   *   *

Section 13.1.4 - Duplicates Not Allowed

Dictionaries cannot have two items with the same key:

Example:
Duplicate values will overwrite existing values:

```
1  car_dict = {
2   "brand": "Acura",
3   "model": "MDX",
4   "year": 2023,
5   "year": 2024
6  }
7  print(car_dict)
```

Section 13.1.5 - Dictionary Length

To determine how many items a dictionary has, use the `len()` function:

Example:
Print the number of items in the dictionary:

```
1  print(len(car_dict))
```

Section 13.1.6 - Dictionary Items - Data Types

The values in dictionary items can be of any data type:

Example:
String, int, boolean, and list data types:

```
1  car_dict = {
2   "brand": "Acura",
3   "electric": False,
4   "year": 2023,
5   "colors": ["red", "white", "blue"]
6  }
```

Section 13.1.7 - `type()`

From Python's perspective, dictionaries are defined as objects with the data type `'dict'`:

```
1  <class 'dict'>
```

Example:

Print the data type of a dictionary:

```
1  car_dict =  {
2    "brand": "Acura",
3    "model": "MDX",
4    "year": 2023,
5  }
6  print(type(car_dict))
```

Section 13.1.8 - The `dict()` Constructor

It is also possible to use the `dict()` constructor to make a dictionary.

Example:

Using the `dict()` method to make a dictionary:

```
1  person_dict = dict(name = "James", age = 25, country = "United States")
2  print(person_dict)
```

Section 13.2 - Access Dictionary Items

Section 13.2.1 - Accessing Items

You can access the items of a dictionary by referring to its key name, inside square brackets:

Example:

Get the value of the `"model"` key:

```
1  car_dict =  {
2    "brand": "Acura",
3    "model": "MDX",
4    "year": 2023,
5  }
6
7  x = car_dict["model"]
8  print(x)
```

There is also a method called get() that will give you the same result:

```
1  x = car_dict.get("model")
```

Section 13.2.2 - Get Keys

The keys() method will return a list of all the keys in the dictionary.

> **Example:**
> Get a list of the keys:

```
1  x = car_dict.keys()
```

The list of the keys is a *view* of the dictionary, meaning that any changes done to the dictionary will be reflected in the keys list.

> **Example:**
> Add a new item to the original dictionary, and see that the keys list gets updated as well:

```
1  car_dict =  {
2    "brand": "Acura",
3    "model": "MDX",
4    "year": 2023,
5  }
6
7  x = car_dict.keys()
8
9  print(x) # before the change
10
11 car_dict["color"] = "pearl"
12
13 print(x) # after the change
```

Section 13.2.3 - Get Values

The `values()` method will return a list of all the values in the dictionary.

Example:

Get a list of the values:

```
1  x = car_dict.values()
```

The list of the values is a *view* of the dictionary, meaning that any changes done to the dictionary will be reflected in the values list.

Example:

Make a change in the original dictionary, and see that the values list gets updated as well:

```
1  car_dict = {
2    "brand": "Acura",
3    "model": "MDX",
4    "year": 2023,
5  }
6
7  x = car_dict.values()
8
9  print(x) # before the change
10
11 car_dict["year"] = "2024"
12
13 print(x) # after the change
```

Example:

Add a new item to the original dictionary, and see that the values list gets updated as well:

```
1  car_dict =  {
2    "brand": "Acura",
3    "model": "MDX",
4    "year": 2023,
5  }
6
7  x = car_dict.values()
8
9  print(x) # before the change
10
11 car_dict["color"] = "grey"
12
13 print(x) # after the change
```

Section 13.2.4 - Get Items

The items() method will return each item in a dictionary, as tuples in a list.

Example:

Get a list of the key: value pairs

```
1  x = car_dict.items()
```

The returned list is a *view* of the items of the dictionary, meaning that any changes done to the dictionary will be reflected in the items list.

Example:

Make a change in the original dictionary, and see that the items list gets updated as well:

```
1  car_dict = {
2      "brand": "Acura",
3      "model": "MDX",
4      "year": 2023,
5  }
6
7  x = car_dict.items()
8
9  print(x)  # before the change
10
11 car_dict["year"] = "2024"
12
13 print(x)  # after the change
```

Example:

Add a new item to the original dictionary, and see that the items list gets updated as well:

```
1  car_dict = {
2      "brand": "Acura",
3      "model": "MDX",
4      "year": 2023,
5  }
6
7  x = car_dict.items()
8
9  print(x)   # before the change
10
11 car_dict["color"] = "grey"
12
13 print(x)   # after the change
```

Section 13.2.5 - Check if Key Exists

To determine if a specified key is present in a dictionary use the in keyword:

Example:

Check if "model" is present in the dictionary:

```
1  car_dict = {
2      "brand": "Acura",
3      "model": "MDX",
4      "year": 2023,
5  }
6
7  if "model" in car_dict:
8      print("Yes, 'model' is one of the keys in the car_dict dictionary")
```

Section 13.3 - Change Dictionary Items

Section 13.3.1 - Change Values

You can change the value of a specific item by referring to its key name:

Example:

Change the "year" to 2024:

```
1  car_dict = {
2      "brand": "Acura",
3      "model": "MDX",
4      "year": 2023,
5  }
6
7  car_dict["year"] = 2024
```

Section 13.3.2 - Update Dictionary

The update() method will update the dictionary with the items from the given argument.

The argument must be a dictionary, or an iterable object with key: value pairs.

Example:

Update the "year" of the car by using the update() method:

```
1  car_dict = {
2      "brand": "Acura",
3      "model": "MDX",
4      "year": 2023,
5  }
6
7  car_dict.update({"year": 2024})
```

Section 13.4 - Add Dictionary Items

Section 13.4.1 - Adding Items

Adding an item to the dictionary is done by using a new index key and assigning a value to it:

Example:

```
1  car_dict = {
2      "brand": "Acura",
3      "model": "MDX",
4      "year": 2023,
5  }
6  car_dict["color"] = "grey"
7  print(car_dict)
```

Section 13.4.2 - Update Dictionary

The update() method will update the dictionary with the items from a given argument. If the item does not exist, the item will be added.

The argument must be a dictionary, or an iterable object with key: value pairs.

> **Example:**
> Add a color item to the dictionary by using the update() method:

```
1  car_dict = {
2      "brand": "Acura",
3      "model": "MDX",
4      "year": 2023,
5  }
6  car_dict.update({"year": 2024})
```

Section 13.5 - Remove Dictionary Items

Section 13.5.1 - Removing Items

There are several methods to remove items from a dictionary:

> **Example:** The pop() method removes the item with the specified key name:

```
1  car_dict = {
2      "brand": "Acura",
3      "model": "MDX",
4      "year": 2023,
5  }
6  car_dict.pop("model")
7    print(car_dict)
```

Example: The `popitem()` method removes the last inserted item (in versions before 3.7, a random item is removed instead):

```
1  car_dict = {
2      "brand": "Acura",
3      "model": "MDX",
4      "year": 2023,
5  }
6  car_dict.popitem()
7    print(car_dict)
```

Example: The `del` keyword removes the item with the specified key name:

```
1  car_dict = {
2      "brand": "Acura",
3      "model": "MDX",
4      "year": 2023,
5  }
6  del car_dict["model"]
7  print(car_dict)
```

Example: The `del` keyword can also delete the dictionary completely:

```
1  car_dict = {
2      "brand": "Acura",
3      "model": "MDX",
4      "year": 2023,
5  }
6  del car_dict
7  print(car_dict) #this will cause an error because "car_dict" no longer exists.
```

Example: The `clear()` method empties the dictionary:

```
1  car_dict = {
2      "brand": "Acura",
3      "model": "MDX",
4      "year": 2023,
5  }
6  car_dict.clear()
7  print(car_dict)
```

Section 13.6 - Loop Dictionaries

Section 13.6.1 - Loop Through a Dictionary

You can loop through a dictionary by using a for loop.

When looping through a dictionary, the return value are the *keys* of the dictionary, but there are methods to return the *values* as well.

Example:

Print all key names in the dictionary, one by one:

```
1  car_dict = {
2      "brand": "Acura",
3      "model": "MDX",
4      "year": 2023,
5  }
6
7  for x in car_dict:
8    print(x)
```

Example:

Print all values in the dictionary, one by one:

```
1   car_dict = {
2       "brand": "Acura",
3       "model": "MDX",
4       "year": 2023,
5   }
6
7   for x in car_dict:
8     print(car_dict[x])
```

Example:

You can also use the `values()` method to return values of a dictionary:

```
1   car_dict = {
2       "brand": "Acura",
3       "model": "MDX",
4       "year": 2023,
5   }
6
7   for x in car_dict.values():
8     print(x)
```

Example:

You can use the `keys()` method to return the keys of a dictionary:

```
1   car_dict = {
2       "brand": "Acura",
3       "model": "MDX",
4       "year": 2023,
5   }
6
7   for x in car_dict.keys():
8     print(x)
```

Example:

Loop through both *keys* and *values*, by using the `items()` method:

```
1  car_dict = {
2      "brand": "Acura",
3      "model": "MDX",
4      "year": 2023,
5  }
6
7  for x, y in car_dict.items():
8    print(x, y)
```

Section 13.7 - Copy Dictionaries

Section 13.7.1 - Copy a Dictionary

You cannot copy a dictionary simply by typing new_car_dict = car_dict, because: new_car_dict will only be a *reference* to car_dict, and changes made in car_dict will automatically also be made in new_car_dict.

There are ways to make a copy, one way is to use the built-in Dictionary method copy().

Example:

Make a copy of a dictionary with the copy() method:

```
1  car_dict = {
2      "brand": "Acura",
3      "model": "MDX",
4      "year": 2023,
5  }
6
7  new_car_dict = car_dict.copy()
8  print(new_car_dict)
```

Another way to make a copy is to use the built-in function dict().

Example:

Make a copy of a dictionary with the copy() method:

```
1   car_dict = {
2       "brand": "Acura",
3       "model": "MDX",
4       "year": 2023,
5   }
6
7   new_car_dict = dict(car_dict)
8   print(new_car_dict)
```

Section 13.8 - Nested Dictionaries

Section 13.8.1 - Nested Dictionaries

A dictionary can contain dictionaries, this is called nested dictionaries.

Example:

Create a dictionary that contain three dictionaries:

```
1   students = {
2     "student1" : {
3       "name" : "John",
4       "year" : "Senior"
5     },
6     "student2" : {
7       "name" : "Sarah",
8       "year" : "Sophomore"
9     },
10    "student3" : {
11      "name" : "Victor",
12      "year" : "Junior"
13    }
14  }
```

Or, if you want to add three dictionaries into a new dictionary:

Example:

Create three dictionaries, then create one dictionary that will contain the other three dictionaries:

```
1   student1 : {
2       "name" : "John",
3       "year" : "Senior"
4   },
5   student2 : {
6       "name" : "Sarah",
7       "year" : "Sophomore"
8   },
9   student3 : {
10      "name" : "Victor",
11      "year" : "Junior"
12  }
13  students = {
14      "student1" : student1,
15      "student2" : student2,
16      "student3" : student3
17  }
```

Section 13.8.2 - Access Items in Nested Dictionaries

To access items from a nested dictionary, you use the name of the dictionaries, starting with the outer dictionary:

Example:

Print the name of student 2:

```
1   print(students["student2"]["name"])
```

Section 13.9 - Dictionary Methods

Python has a set of built-in methods that you can use on dictionaries.

Method	Description
clear()	Removes all the elements from the dictionary
copy()	Returns a copy of the dictionary
fromkeys()	Returns a dictionary with the specified keys and value
get()	Returns the value of the specified key
items()	Returns a list containing a tuple for each key value pair
keys()	Returns a list containing the dictionary's keys
pop()	Removes the element with the specified key
popitem()	Removes the last inserted key-value pair
setdefault()	Returns the value of the specified key. If the key does not exist: insert the key, with the specified value
update()	Updates the dictionary with the specified key-value pairs
values()	Returns a list of all the values in the dictionary

Python If...Else

Section 14.1 - Python Conditions and If statements

Python supports the usual logical conditions from mathematics:

- Equals: a == b
- Not Equals: a != b
- Less than: a < b
- Less than or equal to: a <= b
- Greater than: a > b
- Greater than or equal to: a >= b

These conditions can be used in several ways, most commonly in "if statements" and loops.

An "if statement" is written by using the if keyword.

Example:

If statement:

```
1  a = 35
2  b = 250
3  if b > a:
4    print("b is greater than a")
```

In this example we use two variables, a and b, which are used as part of the if statement to test whether b is greater than a. As a is 35, and b is 250, we know that 250 is greater than 35, and so we print to screen that "b is greater than a".

Section 14.2 - Indentation

Python relies on indentation (whitespace at the beginning of a line) to define scope in the code. Other programming languages often use curly-brackets for this purpose.

Example:

If statement, without indentation (will raise an error):

```
1   a = 35
2   b = 250
3   if b > a:
4   print("b is greater than a")  # you will get an error
```

Section 14.3 - Elif

The elif keyword is Python's way of saying "if the previous conditions were not true, then try this condition".

Example:

```
1   a = 35
2   b = 35
3   if b > a:
4     print("b is greater than a")
5   elif a == b:
6     print("a and b are equal")
```

In this example a is equal to b, so the first condition is not true, but the elif condition is true, so we print to screen that "a and b are equal".

Section 14.4 - Else

The else keyword catches anything which isn't caught by the preceding conditions.

Example:

```
1   a = 250
2   b = 35
3   if b > a:
4     print("b is greater than a")
5   elif a == b:
6     print("a and b are equal")
7   else:
8     print("a is greater than b")
```

In this example a is greater than b, so the first condition is not true, also the elif condition is not true, so we go to the else condition and print to screen that "a is greater than b".

You can also have an else without the elif:

Example:

```
1  a = 250
2  b = 35
3  if b > a:
4    print("b is greater than a")
5  else:
6    print("b is not greater than a")
```

Section 14.5 - Short Hand `If`

If you have only one statement to execute, you can put it on the same line as the `if` statement.

Example:

One line if statement:

```
1  if a > b: print("a is greater than b")
```

Section 14.6 - Short Hand `If ... Else`

If you have only one statement to execute, one for `if`, and one for `else`, you can put it all on the same line:

Example:

One line if else statement:

```
1  a = 5
2  b = 150
3  print("A") if a > b else print("B")
```

Note:

This technique is known as **Ternary Operators**, or **Conditional Expressions**.

You can also have multiple else statements on the same line:

Example:

One line `if else` statement, with 3 conditions:

```
1   a = 250
2   b = 250
3   print("A") if a > b else print("=") if a == b else print("B")
```

Section 14.7 - And

The and keyword is a logical operator, and is used to combine conditional statements:

Example:

Test if a is greater than b, AND if c is greater than a:

```
1   a = 250
2   b = 35
3   c = 500
4   if a > b and c > a:
5     print("Both conditions are True")
```

Section 14.8 - Or

The or keyword is a logical operator, and is used to combine conditional statements:

Example:

Test if a is greater than b, OR if a is greater than c:

```
1   a = 250
2   b = 35
3   c = 500
4   if a > b or a > c:
5     print("At least one of the conditions is True")
```

Section 14.9 - Not

The not keyword is a logical operator, and is used to reverse the result of the conditional statement:

Example:

Test if a is NOT greater than b:

```
1  a = 35
2  b = 250
3  if not a > b:
4    print("a is NOT greater than b")
```

Section 14.10 - Nested If

You can have if statements inside if statements, this is called *nested* if statements.

Example:

```
1  x = 41
2
3  if x > 10:
4    print("Above ten,")
5    if x > 20:
6      print("and also above 20!")
7    else:
8      print("but not above 20.")
```

Section 14.11 - The pass Statement

if statements cannot be empty, but if you for some reason have an if statement with no content, put in the pass statement to avoid getting an error.

Example:

```
1  a = 35
2  b = 250
3
4  if b > a:
5    pass
```

Python While Loops

Section 15.1 - Python Loops

Python has two primitive loop commands:

- while loops
- for loops

Section 15.1.1 - The while Loop

With the while loop we can execute a set of statements as long as a condition is true.

Example:
Print i as long as i is less than 6:

```
1  i = 1
2  while i < 6:
3    print(i)
4    i += 1
```

Note: remember to increment i, or else the loop will continue forever.

The while loop requires relevant variables to be ready, in this example we need to define an indexing variable, i, which we set to 1.

Section 15.1.2 - The break Statement

With the break statement we can stop the loop even if the while condition is true:

Example:
Exit the loop when i is 3:

```
1  i = 1
2  while i < 6:
3    print(i)
4    if i == 3:
5      break
6    i += 1
```

Section 15.1.3 - The continue Statement

With the continue statement we can stop the current iteration, and continue with the next:

Example:

Continue to the next iteration if i is 3:

```
1  i = 0
2  while i < 6:
3    i += 1
4    if i == 3:
5      continue
6    print(i)
```

Section 15.1.4 - The else Statement

With the else statement we can run a block of code once when the condition no longer is true:

Example:

Print a message once the condition is false:

```
1  i = 1
2  while i < 6:
3    print(i)
4    i += 1
5  else:
6    print("i is no longer less than 6")
```

Python For Loops

Section 16.1 - For Loops

A for loop is used for iterating over a sequence (that is either a list, a tuple, a dictionary, a set, or a string).

This is less like the for keyword in other programming languages, and works more like an iterator method as found in other object-orientated programming languages.

With the for loop we can execute a set of statements, once for each item in a list, tuple, set etc.

> **Example:**
> Print each fruit in a fruit list:

```
1  fruits = ["apple", "banana", "cherry"]
2  for fruit in fruits:
3    print(fruit)
```

The for loop does not require an indexing variable to set beforehand.

Section 16.2 - Looping Through a String

Even strings are iterable objects, they contain a sequence of characters:

> **Example:**
> Loop through the letters in the word "banana":

```
1  for x in "banana":
2    print(x)
```

Section 16.3 - The break Statement

With the break statement we can stop the loop before it has looped through all the items:

> **Example:**
> Exit the loop when x is "banana"

```
1  fruits = ["apple", "banana", "cherry"]
2  for fruit in fruits:
3    print(fruit)
4    if fruit == "banana":
5      break
```

Example:

Exit the loop when x is "banana", but this time the break comes before the print:

```
1  fruits = ["apple", "banana", "cherry"]
2  for fruit in fruits:
3    if fruit == "banana":
4      break
5    print(fruit)
```

Section 16.4 - The continue Statement

With the continue statement we can stop the current iteration of the loop, and continue with the next:

Example:

Do not print banana:

```
1  fruits = ["apple", "banana", "cherry"]
2  for fruit in fruits:
3    if fruit == "banana":
4      continue
5    print(fruit)
```

Section 16.5 - The range() Function

To loop through a set of code a specified number of times, we can use the range() function,

The range() function returns a sequence of numbers, starting from 0 by default, and increments by 1 (by default), and ends at a specified number.

Example:

Using the range() function:

```
1  for x in range(6):
2    print(x)
```

Note that range(6) is not the values of 0 to 6, but the values 0 to 5.

The range() function defaults to 0 as a starting value, however it is possible to specify the starting value by adding a parameter: range(2, 6), which means values from 2 to 6 (but not including 6):

Example:
Using the start parameter:

```
1  for x in range(2, 6):
2    print(x)
```

The range() function defaults to increment the sequence by 1, however it is possible to specify the increment value by adding a third parameter: range(2, 30, 3):

Example:
Increment the sequence with 3 (default is 1):

```
1  for x in range(2, 30, 3):
2    print(x)
```

Section 16.6 - Else in For Loop

The else keyword in a for loop specifies a block of code to be executed when the loop is finished:

Example:
Print all numbers from 0 to 5, and print a message when the loop has ended:

```
1  for x in range(6):
2    print(x)
3  else:
4    print("Finally finished!")
```

Note: The else block will NOT be executed if the loop is stopped by a break statement.

Example:
Break the loop when x is 3, and see what happens with the else block:

```
1  for x in range(6):
2    if x == 3: break
3    print(x)
4  else:
5    print("Finally finished!")
```

Section 16.7 - Nested Loops

A nested loop is a loop inside a loop.

The "inner loop" will be executed one time for each iteration of the "outer loop":

Example:

Print each adjective for every fruit:

```
1  adj = ["red", "big", "tasty"]
2  fruits = ["apple", "banana", "cherry"]
3
4  for x in adj:
5    for y in fruits:
6      print(x, y)
```

Section 16.8 - The pass Statement

for loops cannot be empty, but if you for some reason have a for loop with no content, put in the pass statement to avoid getting an error.

Example:

```
1  for x in [0, 1, 2]:
2    pass
```

Python Functions

A function is a block of code which only runs when it is called.

You can pass data, known as parameters, into a function.

A function can return data as a result.

Section 17.1 - Creating a Function

In Python a function is defined using the `def` keyword:

Example:

```python
1  def my_function():
2    print("Hello from a function")
```

Section 17.2 - Calling a Function

To call a function, use the function name followed by parenthesis:

Example:

```python
1  def my_function():
2    print("Hello from a function")
3
4  my_function()
```

Section 17.3 - Arguments

Information can be passed into functions as arguments.

Arguments are specified after the function name, inside the parentheses. You can add as many arguments as you want, just separate them with a comma.

The following example has a function with one argument (`first_name`). When the function is called, we pass along a first name, which is used inside the function to print the full name:

Example:

```
1  def my_function(first_name):
2     print(first_name + " Smith")
3
4  my_function("Harrison")
5  my_function("Jennifer")
6  my_function("Andrew")
```

Arguments are often shortened to *args* in Python documentation[1].

Section 17.4 - Parameters or Arguments?

The terms *parameter* and *argument* can be used for the same thing: information that are passed into a function.

From a function's perspective:

- A parameter is the variable listed inside the parentheses in the function definition.
- An argument is the value that is sent to the function when it is called.

Section 17.4.1 - Number of Arguments

By default, a function must be called with the correct number of arguments. Meaning that if your function expects 2 arguments, you have to call the function with 2 arguments, not more, and not less.

Example:

This function expects 2 arguments, and gets 2 arguments:

```
1  def my_function(first_name, last_name):
2     print(first_name + " " + last_name)
3
4  my_function("Harrison", "Smith")
```

If you try to call the function with 1 or 3 arguments, you will get an error:

Example:

This function expects 2 arguments, but gets only 1:

---

[1]https://docs.python.org/3/index.html

```
1  def my_function(first_name, last_name):
2    print(first_name + " " + last_name)
3
4  my_function("Harrison")
```

Section 17.4.2 - Arbitrary Arguments, *args

If you do not know how many arguments that will be passed into your function, add a * before the parameter name in the function definition.

This way the function will receive a *tuple* of arguments, and can access the items accordingly:

> **Example:**
> If the number of arguments is unknown, add a * before the parameter name:

```
1  def my_function(*kids):
2    print("The youngest child is " + kids[2])
3
4  my_function("Harrison", "Jennefer", "Andrew")
```

Arbitrary Arguments are often shortened to *args* in Python documentation.

Section 17.4.3 - Keyword Arguments

You can also send arguments with the *key = value* syntax.

This way the order of the arguments does not matter.

Example

```
1  def my_function(child3, child2, child1):
2    print("The youngest child is " + child3)
3
4  my_function(child1 = "Harrison", child2 = "Jennifer", child3 = "Andrew")
```

The phrase *Keyword Arguments* are often shortened to *kwargs* in Python documentations

Section 17.4.4 - Arbitrary Keyword Arguments, **kwargs

If you do not know how many keyword arguments that will be passed into your function, add two asterisk: ** before the parameter name in the function definition.

This way the function will receive a *dictionary* of arguments, and can access the items accordingly:

Example:

If the number of keyword arguments is unknown, add a double ** before the parameter name:

```
1  def my_function(**kid):
2    print("His last name is " + kid["last_name"])
3
4  my_function(first_name = "Harrison", last_name = "Smith")
```

Arbitrary keyword Arguments are often shortened to ***kwargs* in Python documentation.

Section 17.4.5 - Default Parameter Value

The following example shows how to use a default parameter value.

If we call the function without argument, it uses the default value:

Example:

```
1  def my_function(country = "United States of America"):
2    print("I am from " + country)
3
4  my_function("Barbados")
5  my_function("South Africa")
6  my_function()
7  my_function("Colombia")
```

Section 17.4.6 - Passing a List as an Argument

You can send any data types of argument to a function (string, number, list, dictionary etc.), and it will be treated as the same data type inside the function.

E.g. if you send a List as an argument, it will still be a List when it reaches the function:

Example:

```
1   def my_function(food):
2     for x in food:
3       print(x)
4
5   fruits = ["apple", "banana", "cherry"]
6
7   my_function(fruits)
```

Section 17.4.7 - Return Values

To let a function return a value, use the `return` statement:

> Example:

```
1   def my_function(x):
2     return 5 * x
3
4   print(my_function(3))
5   print(my_function(5))
6   print(my_function(9))
```

Section 17.4.8 - The pass Statement

`function` definitions cannot be empty, but if you for some reason have a `function` definition with no content, put in the `pass` statement to avoid getting an error.

> Example:

```
1   def myfunction():
2     pass
```

Section 17.5 - Recursion

Python also accepts function recursion, which means a defined function can call itself.

Recursion is a common mathematical and programming concept. It means that a function calls itself. This has the benefit of meaning that you can loop through data to reach a result.

The developer should be very careful with recursion as it can be quite easy to slip into writing a function which never terminates, or one that uses excess amounts of memory or processor power. However, when written correctly recursion can be a very efficient and mathematically-elegant approach to programming.

In this example, `tri_recursion()` is a function that we have defined to call itself ("recurse"). We use the k variable as the data, which decrements (-1) every time we recurse. The recursion ends when the condition is not greater than 0 (i.e. when it is 0).

To a new developer it can take some time to work out how exactly this works, best way to find out is by testing and modifying it.

Example:

Recursion Example

```python
def tri_recursion(k):
  if(k > 0):
    result = k + tri_recursion(k - 1)
    print(result)
  else:
    result = 0
  return result

print("\n\nRecursion Example Results")
tri_recursion(6)
```

Python Lambda

A lambda function is a small anonymous function.

A lambda function can take any number of arguments, but can only have one expression.

Section 18.1 - Syntax

```
lambda *arguments* : *expression*
```

The expression is executed and the result is returned:

Example:

Add 10 to argument a, and return the result:

```
1  x = lambda a : a + 10
2  print(x(5))
```

Lambda functions can take any number of arguments:

Example:

Multiply argument a with argument b and return the result:

```
1  x = lambda a, b : a * b
2  print(x(5, 6))
```

Example:

Summarize argument a, b, and c and return the result:

```
1  x = lambda a, b, c : a + b + c
2  print(x(5, 6, 2))
```

Section 18.2 - Why Use Lambda Functions?

The power of lambda is better shown when you use them as an anonymous function inside another function.

Say you have a function definition that takes one argument, and that argument will be multiplied with an unknown number:

123

```
1  def myfunc(n):
2    return lambda a : a * n
```

Use that function definition to make a function that always doubles the number you send in:

Example:

```
1  def myfunc(n):
2    return lambda a : a * n
3
4  mydoubler = myfunc(2)
5
6  print(mydoubler(11))
```

Or, use the same function definition to make a function that always *triples* the number you send in:

Example:

```
1  def myfunc(n):
2    return lambda a : a * n
3
4  mytripler = myfunc(3)
5
6  print(mytripler(11))
```

Or, use the same function definition to make both functions, in the same program:

Example:

```
1  def myfunc(n):
2    return lambda a : a * n
3
4  mydoubler = myfunc(2)
5  mytripler = myfunc(3)
6
7  print(mydoubler(11))
8  print(mytripler(11))
```

Use lambda functions when an anonymous function is required for a short period of time.

Python Arrays

Note: Python does not have built-in support for Arrays, but Python Lists can be used instead.

Section 19.1 - Arrays

Note: This page shows you how to use lists as arrays, however, to work with arrays in Python you will have to import a library, like the NumPy library[1].

Arrays are used to store multiple values in one single variable:

Example:

Create an array containing car names:

```
1  cars = ["Ford", "Volvo", "BMW"]
```

Section 19.1.1 - What is an Array?

An array is a special variable, which can hold more than one value at a time.

If you have a list of items (a list of car names, for example), storing the cars in single variables could look like this:

```
car1 = "Ford" car2 = "Volvo" car3 = "BMW"
```

However, what if you want to loop through the cars and find a specific one? And what if you had not 3 cars, but 300?

The solution is an array!

An array can hold many values under a single name, and you can access the values by referring to an index number.

Section 19.1.2 - Access the Elements of an Array

You refer to an array element by referring to the *index number*.

Example:

Get the value of the first array item:

---

[1]https://numpy.org/

125

```
1   x = cars[0]
2   print(x)
```

Example:
Modify the value of the first array item:

```
1   cars[0] = "Toyota"
2   print(x)
```

Section 19.1.3 - The Length of an Array

Use the len() method to return the length of an array (the number of elements in an array).

Example:
Return the number of elements in the cars array:

```
1   x = len(cars)
2   print(x)
```

Note: The length of an array is always one more than the highest array index.

Section 19.1.4 - Looping Array Elements

You can use the for in loop to loop through all the elements of an array.

Example:
Print each item in the cars array:

```
1   for x in cars:
2       print(x)
```

Section 19.1.5 - Adding Array Elements

You can use the append() method to add an element to an array.

Example:
Add one more element to the cars array:

```
1   cars.append("Honda")
2   print(cars)
```

Section 19.1.6 - Removing Array Elements

You can use the `pop()` method to remove an element from the array.

Example:

Delete the second element of the `cars` array:

```
1   cars.pop(1)
2   print(cars)
```

You can also use the `remove()` method to remove an element from the array.

Example:

Delete the element that has the value "Volvo":

```
1   cars.remove("Volvo")
2   print(cars)
```

Note: The list's `remove()` method only removes the first occurrence of the specified value.

Section 19.2 - Array Methods

Python has a set of built-in methods that you can use on lists/arrays.

Method	Description
append()	Adds an element at the end of the list
clear()	Removes all the elements from the list
copy()	Returns a copy of the list
count()	Returns the number of elements with the specified value
extend()	Add the elements of a list (or any iterable), to the end of the current list
index()	Returns the index of the first element with the specified value
insert()	Adds an element at the specified position

Method	Description
pop( )	Removes the element at the specified position
remove( )	Removes the first item with the specified value
reverse( )	Reverses the order of the list
sort( )	Sorts the list

Note: Python does not have built-in support for Arrays, but Python Lists can be used instead.

Python Classes and Objects

Section 20.1 - Python Classes/Objects

Python is an object oriented programming language.

Almost everything in Python is an object, with its properties and methods.

A Class is like an object constructor, or a "blueprint" for creating objects.

Section 20.1.1 - Create a Class

To create a class, use the keyword class:

Example:

Create a class named MyClass, with a property named x

```
1  class MyClass:
2      x = 5
```

Section 20.1.2 - Create Object

Now we can use the class named MyClass to create objects:

Example:

Create an object named p1, and print the value of x:

```
1  p1 = MyClass()
2  print(p1.x)
```

Section 20.1.3 - The __init__() Function

The examples above are classes and objects in their simplest form, and are not really useful in real life applications.

To understand the meaning of classes we have to understand the built-in __init__() function.

All classes have a function called __init__(), which is always executed when the class is being initiated.

Use the __init__() function to assign values to object properties, or other operations that are necessary to do when the object is being created:

Example:

Create a class named Person, use the __init__() function to assign values for name and age:

```python
class Person:
  def __init__(self, name, age):
    self.name = name
    self.age = age

p1 = Person("John", 36)

print(p1.name)
print(p1.age)
```

Note: The __init__() function is called automatically every time the class is being used to create a new object.

Section 20.1.4 - The __str__() Function

The __str__() function controls what should be returned when the class object is represented as a string.

If the __str__() function is not set, the string representation of the object is returned:

Example:

The string representation of an object WITHOUT the __str__() function:

```
1   class Person:
2     def __init__(self, name, age):
3       self.name = name
4       self.age = age
5
6   p1 = Person("John", 36)
7
8   print(p1)
```

Example:

The string representation of an object WITH the __str__() function:

```
1   class Person:
2     def __init__(self, name, age):
3       self.name = name
4       self.age = age
5
6     def __str__(self):
7       return f"{self.name}({self.age})"
8
9   p1 = Person("John", 36)
10
11  print(p1)
```

Section 20.1.5 - Object Methods

Objects can also contain methods. Methods in objects are functions that belong to the object.

Let us create a method in the Person class:

Example:

Insert a function that prints a greeting, and execute it on the p1 object:

```python
1  class Person:
2    def __init__(self, name, age):
3      self.name = name
4      self.age = age
5
6    def myfunc(self):
7      print("Hello my name is " + self.name)
8
9  p1 = Person("John", 36)
10 p1.myfunc()
```

Note: The self parameter is a reference to the current instance of the class, and is used to access variables that belong to the class.

Section 20.1.6 - The self Parameter

The self parameter is a reference to the current instance of the class, and is used to access variables that belongs to the class.

It does not have to be named self , you can call it whatever you like, but it has to be the first parameter of any function in the class:

Example:

Use the words *anysillyobject* and *abc* instead of *self*:

```python
1  class Person:
2    def __init__(anysillyobject, name, age):
3      anysillyobject.name = name
4      anysillyobject.age = age
5
6    def myfunc(abc):
7      print("Hello my name is " + abc.name)
8
9  p1 = Person("John", 36)
10 p1.myfunc()
```

Section 20.1.7 - Modify Object Properties

You can modify properties on objects like this:

Example:

Set the age of p1 to 40:

```
1  p1.age = 40
```

Section 20.1.8 - Delete Object Properties

You can delete properties on objects by using the `del` keyword:

Example:
Delete the age property from the p1 object:

```
1  del p1.age
```

Section 20.1.9 - Delete Objects

You can delete objects by using the `del` keyword:

Example:
Delete the p1 object:

```
1  del p1
```

Section 20.1.10 - The pass Statement

`class` definitions cannot be empty, but if you for some reason have a `class` definition with no content, put in the pass statement to avoid getting an error.

Example:

```
1  class Person:
2    pass
```

Python Inheritance

Section 21.1 - Python Inheritance

Inheritance allows us to define a class that inherits all the methods and properties from another class.

Parent class is the class being inherited from, also called base class.

Child class is the class that inherits from another class, also called derived class.

Section 21.1.1 - Create a Parent Class

Any class can be a parent class, so the syntax is the same as creating any other class:

Example:

Create a class named Person, with first_name and last_name properties, and a print_name method:

```
1   class Person:
2     def __init__(self, fname, lname):
3       self.first_name = fname
4       self.last_name = lname
5
6     def print_name(self):
7       print(self.firstname, self.lastname)
8
9   # Use the Person class to create an object, and then execute the print_name method:
10
11  x = Person("John", "Doe")
12  x.print_name()
```

Section 21.1.2 - Create a Child Class

To create a class that inherits the functionality from another class, send the parent class as a parameter when creating the child class:

Example:

Create a class named Student, which will inherit the properties and methods from the Person class:

135

```
1   class Student(Person):
2     pass
```

Note: Use the pass keyword when you do not want to add any other properties or methods to the class.

Now the Student class has the same properties and methods as the Person class.

> **Example:**
> Use the Student class to create an object, and then execute the print_name method:

```
1   x = Student("John", "Appleseed")
2   x.print_name()
```

Section 21.1.3 - Add the init() Function

So far we have created a child class that inherits the properties and methods from its parent.

We want to add the __init__() function to the child class (instead of the pass keyword).

Note: The __init__() function is called automatically every time the class is being used to create a new object.

> **Example:**
> Add the __init__() function to the Student class:

```
1   class Student(Person):
2     def __init__(self, fname, lname):
3       # add properties etc.
```

When you add the __init__() function, the child class will no longer inherit the parent's __init__() function.

> **Note:** The child's __init__() function **overrides** the inheritance of the parent's __init__() function.

To keep the inheritance of the parent's __init__() function, add a call to the parent's __init__() function:

> **Example:**

```
1  class Student(Person):
2    def __init__(self, fname, lname):
3      Person.__init__(self, fname, lname)
```

Now we have successfully added the __init__() function, and kept the inheritance of the parent class, and we are ready to add functionality in the __init__() function.

Section 21.1.4 - Use the super() Function

Python also has a super() function that will make the child class inherit all the methods and properties from its parent:

Example:

```
1  class Student(Person):
2    def __init__(self, fname, lname):
3      super().__init__(fname, lname)
```

By using the super() function, you do not have to use the name of the parent element, it will automatically inherit the methods and properties from its parent.

Section 21.1.5 - Add Properties

Example:

Add a property called graduation_year to the Student class:

```
1  class Student(Person):
2    def __init__(self, fname, lname):
3      super().__init__(fname, lname)
4      self.graduation_year = 2023
```

In the example below, the year 2023 should be a variable, and passed into the Student class when creating student objects. To do so, add another parameter in the __init__() function:

Example:

Add a year parameter, and pass the correct year when creating objects:

```
1  class Student(Person):
2    def __init__(self, fname, lname, year):
3      super().__init__(fname, lname)
4      self.graduation_year = year
5
6  x = Student("John", "Appleseed", 2023)
```

Section 21.1.6 - Add Methods

Example:

Add a method called welcome to the Student class:

```
1  class Student(Person):
2    def __init__(self, fname, lname, year):
3      super().__init__(fname, lname)
4      self.graduation_year = year
5
6    def welcome(self):
7      print("Welcome", self.first_name, self.last_name, "to the class of", self.gradua\
8  tion_year)
```

If you add a method in the child class with the same name as a function in the parent class, the inheritance of the parent method will be overridden.

Python Iterators

Section 22.1 - Python Iterators

An iterator is an object that contains a countable number of values.

An iterator is an object that can be iterated upon, meaning that you can traverse through all the values.

Technically, in Python, an iterator is an object which implements the iterator protocol, which consist of the methods __iter__() and __next__().

Section 22.1.1 - Iterator vs Iterable

Lists, tuples, dictionaries, and sets are all iterable objects. They are iterable *containers* which you can get an iterator from.

All these objects have a iter() method which is used to get an iterator:

Example:

Return an iterator from a tuple, and print each value:

```
1   fruits_tuple = ("apple", "banana", "cherry")
2   my_it = iter(fruits_tuple)
3
4   print(next(my_it))
5   print(next(my_it))
6   print(next(my_it))
```

Even strings are iterable objects, and can return an iterator:

Example:

Strings are also iterable objects, containing a sequence of characters:

```
1  my_str = "banana"
2  my_it = iter(my_str)
3
4  print(next(my_it))
5  print(next(my_it))
6  print(next(my_it))
7  print(next(my_it))
8  print(next(my_it))
9  print(next(my_it))
```

Section 22.1.2 - Looping Through an Iterator

We can also use a for loop to iterate through an iterable object:

Example:

Iterate the values of a tuple:

```
1  fruits_tuple = ("apple", "banana", "cherry")
2
3  for x in fruits_tuple:
4    print(x)
```

Example:

Iterate the characters of a string:

```
1  my_str = "banana"
2
3  for x in my_str:
4    print(x)
```

The for loop actually creates an iterator object and executes the next() method for each loop.

Section 22.1.3 - Create an Iterator

To create an object/class as an iterator you have to implement the methods __iter__() and __next__() to your object.

As you have learned in the Python Classes/Objects chapter, all classes have a function called __init__(), which allows you to do some initializing when the object is being created.

The __iter__() method acts similar, you can do operations (initializing etc.), but must always return the iterator object itself.

The __next__() method also allows you to do operations, and must return the next item in the sequence.

Example:

Create an iterator that returns numbers, starting with 1, and each sequence will increase by one (returning 1,2,3,4,5 etc.):

```
1   class MyNumbers:
2     def __iter__(self):
3       self.a = 1
4       return self
5
6     def __next__(self):
7       x = self.a
8       self.a += 1
9       return x
10
11  my_class = MyNumbers()
12  my_iter = iter(my_class)
13
14  print(next(my_iter))
15  print(next(my_iter))
16  print(next(my_iter))
17  print(next(my_iter))
18  print(next(my_iter))
```

Section 22.1.4 - StopIteration

The example above would continue forever if you had enough next() statements, or if it was used in a for loop.

To prevent the iteration from going on forever, we can use the StopIteration statement.

In the __next__() method, we can add a terminating condition to raise an error if the iteration is done a specified number of times:

Example:

Stop after 20 iterations:

```
1   class MyNumbers:
2     def __iter__(self):
3       self.a = 1
4       return self
5
6     def __next__(self):
7       if self.a <= 20:
8         x = self.a
9         self.a += 1
10        return x
11      else:
12        raise StopIteration
13
14  my_class = MyNumbers()
15  my_iter = iter(my_class)
16
17  for x in my_iter:
18    print(x)
```

Python Polymorphism

The word "polymorphism" means "many forms", and in programming it refers to methods/functions/operators with the same name that can be executed on many objects or classes.

Section 23.1 - Function Polymorphism

An example of a Python function that can be used on different objects is the len() function.

Section 23.1.1 - String

For strings len() returns the number of characters:

> **Example:**

```
1  x = "Hello Python!"
2
3  print(len(x))
```

Section 23.1.2 - Tuple

For tuples len() returns the number of items in the tuple:

> **Example:**

```
1  fruits_tuple = ("apple", "banana", "cherry")
2
3  print(len(fruits_tuple))
```

Section 23.1.3 - Dictionary

For dictionaries len() returns the number of key/value pairs in the dictionary:

> **Example:**

```
1  cars_dict = {
2    "brand": "Acura",
3    "model": "MDX",
4    "year": 2023
5  }
6
7  print(len(cars_dict))
```

Section 23.2 - Class Polymorphism

Polymorphism is often used in Class methods, where we can have multiple classes with the same method name.

For example, say we have three classes: Car, Boat, and Plane, and they all have a method called move():

Example:

Different classes with the same method:

```
1  class Car:
2    def __init__(self, brand, model):
3      self.brand = brand
4      self.model = model
5
6    def move(self):
7      print("Drive!")
8
9  class Boat:
10   def __init__(self, brand, model):
11     self.brand = brand
12     self.model = model
13
14   def move(self):
15     print("Sail!")
16
17 class Plane:
18   def __init__(self, brand, model):
19     self.brand = brand
20     self.model = model
21
```

```
22    def move(self):
23      print("Fly!")
24
25  car1 = Car("Acura", "MDX")          # Create a Car class
26  boat1 = Boat("Ibiza", "Touring 20")  # Create a Boat class
27  plane1 = Plane("Boeing", "747")     # Create a Plane class
28
29  for x in (car1, boat1, plane1):
30    x.move()
```

Look at the for loop at the end. Because of polymorphism we can execute the same method for all three classes.

Section 23.3 - Inheritance Class Polymorphism

What about classes with child classes with the same name? Can we use polymorphism there?

Yes. If we use the example above and make a parent class called Vehicle, and make Car, Boat, Plane child classes of Vehicle, the child classes inherits the Vehicle methods, but can override them:

Example:

Create a class called Vehicle and make Car, Boat, Plane child classes of Vehicle:

```
1   class Vehicle:
2     def __init__(self, brand, model):
3       self.brand = brand
4       self.model = model
5
6     def move(self):
7       print("Move!")
8
9   class Car(Vehicle):
10    pass
11
12  class Boat(Vehicle):
13    def move(self):
14      print("Sail!")
15
16  class Plane(Vehicle):
17    def move(self):
18      print("Fly!")
```

```
19
20  car1 = Car("Acura", "MDX")         # Create a Car object
21  boat1 = Boat("Ibiza", "Touring 20") # Create a Boat object
22  plane1 = Plane("Boeing", "747")    # Create a Plane object
23
24  for x in (car1, boat1, plane1):
25    print(x.brand)
26    print(x.model)
27    x.move()
```

Child classes inherits the properties and methods from the parent class.

In the example above you can see that the Car class is empty, but it inherits brand, model, and move() from Vehicle.

The Boat and Plane classes also inherit brand, model, and move() from Vehicle, but they both override the move() method.

Because of polymorphism we can execute the same method for all classes.

Python Scope

A variable is only available from inside the region it is created. This is called **scope**.

Section 24.1 - Local Scope

A variable created inside a function belongs to the *local scope* of that function, and can only be used inside that function.

Example:

A variable created inside a function is available inside that function:

```
1  def my_func():
2    x = 300
3    print(x)
4
5  my_func()
```

Section 24.1.1 - Function Inside Function

As explained in the example above, the variable x is not available outside the function, but it is available for any function inside the function:

Example:

The local variable can be accessed from a function within the function:

```
1  def my_func():
2    x = 300
3    def my_inner_func():
4      print(x)
5    my_inner_func()
6
7  my_func()
```

Section 24.2 - Global Scope

A variable created in the main body of the Python code is a global variable and belongs to the global scope.

Global variables are available from within any scope, global and local.

> **Example:**
> A variable created outside of a function is global and can be used by anyone:

```
1   x = 300
2
3   def my_func():
4       print(x)
5
6   my_func()
7
8   print(x)
```

Section 24.2.1 - Naming Variables

If you operate with the same variable name inside and outside of a function, Python will treat them as two separate variables, one available in the global scope (outside the function) and one available in the local scope (inside the function):

> **Example:**
> The function will print the local x, and then the code will print the global x:

```
1   x = 300
2
3   def my_func():
4       x = 200
5       print(x)
6
7   my_func()
8
9   print(x)
```

Section 24.3 - Global Keyword

If you need to create a global variable, but are stuck in the local scope, you can use the global keyword.

The global keyword makes the variable global.

Example:

If you use the global keyword, the variable belongs to the global scope:

```
1  def my_func():
2    global x
3    x = 300
4
5  my_func()
6
7  print(x)
```

Also, use the global keyword if you want to make a change to a global variable inside a function.

Example:

To change the value of a global variable inside a function, refer to the variable by using the global keyword:

```
1  x = 300
2
3  def my_func():
4    global x
5    x = 200
6
7  my_func()
8
9  print(x)
```

Python Modules

Section 25.1 - What is a Module?

Consider a module to be the same as a code library.

A file containing a set of functions you want to include in your application.

Section 25.1.1 - Create a Module

To create a module just save the code you want in a file with the file extension .py:

> **Example:**
>
> Save this code in a file named my_module.py

```
1  def greeting(name):
2    print("Hello, " + name)
```

Section 25.1.2 - Use a Module

Now we can use the module we just created, by using the import statement:

> **Example:**
>
> Import the module named my_module, and call the greeting function:

```
1  import my_module
2
3  my_module.greeting("Johnny")
```

> **Note:** When using a function from a module, use the syntax: *module_name.function_-name.*

Section 25.1.3 - Variables in Module

The module can contain functions, as already described, but also variables of all types (arrays, dictionaries, objects etc):

> **Example:**
> Save this code in the file my_module.py

```
1  person1 = {
2    "name": "George",
3    "age": 36,
4    "country": "Bahamas"
5  }
```

Example

Import the module named `my_module`, and access the `person1` dictionary:

```
1  import my_module
2
3  a = my_module.person1["age"]
4  print(a)
```

Section 25.1.4 - Naming a Module

You can name the module file whatever you like, but it must have the file extension `.py`

Section 25.1.5 - Re-naming a Module

You can create an alias when you import a module, by using the `as` keyword:

Example:

Create an alias for `my_module` called `mx`:

```
1  import my_module as mx
2
3  a = mx.person1["age"]
4  print(a)
```

Section 25.1.6 - Built-in Modules

There are several built-in modules in Python, which you can import whenever you like.

Example:

Import and use the `platform` module:

```
1   import platform
2
3   x = platform.system()
4   print(x)
```

Section 25.1.7 - Using the `dir()` Function

There is a built-in function to list all the function names (or variable names) in a module. The `dir()` function:

> **Example:**
>
> List all the defined names belonging to the platform module:

```
1   import platform
2
3   x = dir(platform)
4   print(x)
```

Note: The `dir()` function can be used on *all* modules, also the ones you create yourself.

Section 25.1.8 - Import From Module

You can choose to import only parts from a module, by using the `from` keyword.

> **Example:**
>
> The module named `my_module` has one function and one dictionary:

```
1   def greeting(name):
2     print("Hello, " + name)
3
4   person1 = {
5     "name": "George",
6     "age": 36,
7     "country": "Bahamas"
8   }
```

> **Example:**
>
> Import only the `person1` dictionary from the module:

```
1   from my_module import person1
2
3   print (person1["age"])
```

Note: When importing using the `from` keyword, do not use the module name when referring to elements in the module. Example: `person1["age"]`, **not** ~~my_module.person1["age"]~~

Python Datetime

Section 26.1 - Python Dates

A date in Python is not a data type of its own, but we can import a module named datetime to work with dates as date objects.

Example:

Import the datetime module and display the current date:

```python
import datetime

x = datetime.datetime.now()
print(x)
```

Section 26.2 - Date Output

When we execute the code from the example above the result will be:

```
2023-09-30 23:24:20.625917
```

The date contains year, month, day, hour, minute, second, and microsecond.

The datetime module has many methods to return information about the date object.

Here are a few examples, you will learn more about them later in this chapter:

Example:

Return the year and name of weekday:

```
1  import datetime
2
3  x = datetime.datetime.now()
4
5  print(x.year)
6  print(x.strftime("%A"))
```

Section 26.3 - Creating Date Objects

To create a date, we can use the `datetime()` class (constructor) of the `datetime` module.

The `datetime()` class requires three parameters to create a date: year, month, day.

> **Example:**
> Create a date object:

```
1  import datetime
2
3  x = datetime.datetime(2020, 5, 17)
4
5  print(x)
```

The `datetime()` class also takes parameters for time and timezone (hour, minute, second, microsecond, tzone), but they are optional, and has a default value of `0`, (`None` for timezone).

Section 26.4 - The `strftime()` Method

The `datetime` object has a method for formatting date objects into readable strings.

The method is called `strftime()`, and takes one parameter, `format`, to specify the format of the returned string:

> **Example:**
> Display the name of the month:

```
1  import datetime
2
3  x = datetime.datetime(2023, 9, 1)
4
5  print(x.strftime("%B"))
```

A reference of all the legal format codes:

Directive	Description	Example
%a	Weekday, short version	Wed
%A	Weekday, full version	Wednesday
%w	Weekday as a number 0-6, 0 is Sunday	3
%d	Day of month 01-31	31
%b	Month name, short version	Dec
%B	Month name, full version	December
%m	Month as a number 01-12	12
%y	Year, short version, without century	18
%Y	Year, full version	2023
%H	Hour 00-23	17
%I	Hour 00-12	05
%p	AM/PM	PM
%M	Minute 00-59	41
%S	Second 00-59	08
%f	Microsecond 000000-999999	548513
%z	UTC offset	+0100
%Z	Timezone	CST
%j	Day number of year 001-366	365
%U	Week number of year, Sunday as the first day of week, 00-53	52
%W	Week number of year, Monday as the first day of week, 00-53	52
%c	Local version of date and time	Mon Dec 31 17:41:00 2023
%C	Century	20
%x	Local version of date	12/31/23
%X	Local version of time	17:41:00
%%	A % character	%
%G	ISO 8601 year	2023
%u	ISO 8601 weekday (1-7)	1
%V	ISO 8601 weeknumber (01-53)	01

Python Math

Python has a set of built-in math functions, including an extensive math module, that allows you to perform mathematical tasks on numbers.

Section 27.1 - Built-in Math Functions

The min() and max() functions can be used to find the lowest or highest value in an iterable:

Example:

```
1  x = min(5, 10, 25)
2  y = max(5, 10, 25)
3
4  print(x)
5  print(y)
```

The abs() function returns the absolute (positive) value of the specified number:

Example:

```
1  x = abs(-7.25)
2
3  print(x)
```

The pow(*x*, *y*) function returns the value of x to the power of y (x^y).

Example:
Return the value of 4 to the power of 3 (same as 4 * 4 * 4):

```
1  x = pow(4, 3)
2
3  print(x)
```

Section 27.2 - The Math Module

Python has also a built-in module called math, which extends the list of mathematical functions.

To use it, you must import the math module:

import math

When you have imported the math module, you can start using methods and constants of the module.

The math.sqrt() method for example, returns the square root of a number:

Example:

```
1  import math
2
3  x = math.sqrt(64)
4
5  print(x)
```

The math.ceil() method rounds a number upwards to its nearest integer, and the math.floor() method rounds a number downwards to its nearest integer, and returns the result:

Example:

```
1  import math
2
3  x = math.ceil(1.4)
4  y = math.floor(1.4)
5
6  print(x) # returns 2
7  print(y) # returns 1
```

The math.pi constant, returns the value of PI (3.14...):

Example:

```
1   import math
2
3   x = math.pi
4
5   print(x)
```

Python JSON

JSON is a syntax for storing and exchanging data.

JSON is text, written with JavaScript object notation.

Section 28.1 - JSON in Python

Python has a built-in package called json, which can be used to work with JSON data.

> **Example:**
> Import the json module:

```
1  import json
```

Section 28.2 - Parse JSON - Convert from JSON to Python

If you have a JSON string, you can parse it by using the json.loads() method.

The result will be a Python dictionary.

> **Example:**
> Convert from JSON to Python:

```
1  import json
2
3  # some JSON:
4  x =  '{ "name":"Harrison", "age":30, "city":"Florida"}'
5
6  # parse x:
7  y = json.loads(x)
8
9  # the result is a Python dictionary:
10 print(y["age"])
```

Section 28.3 - Convert from Python to JSON

If you have a Python object, you can convert it into a JSON string by using the `json.dumps()` method.

Example:

Convert from Python to JSON:

```
1   import json
2
3   # a Python object (dict):
4   x = {
5     "name": "Harrison",
6     "age": 30,
7     "city": "Florida"
8   }
9
10  # convert into JSON:
11  y = json.dumps(x)
12
13  # the result is a JSON string:
14  print(y)
```

You can convert Python objects of the following types, into JSON strings:

- dict
- list
- tuple
- string
- int
- float
- True
- False
- None

Example:

Convert Python objects into JSON strings, and print the values:

```
 1  import json
 2
 3  print(json.dumps({"name": "Harrison", "age": 30}))
 4  print(json.dumps(["apple", "bananas"]))
 5  print(json.dumps(("kiwi", "pineapple")))
 6  print(json.dumps("hello"))
 7  print(json.dumps(52))
 8  print(json.dumps(31.76))
 9  print(json.dumps(True))
10  print(json.dumps(False))
11  print(json.dumps(None))
```

When you convert from Python to JSON, Python objects are converted into the JSON (JavaScript) equivalent:

Python	JSON
dict	Object
list	Array
tuple	Array
str	String
int	Number
float	Number
True	true
False	false
None	null

Example:

Convert a Python object containing all the legal data types:

```
 1  import json
 2
 3  x = {
 4    "name": "Harrison",
 5    "age": 30,
 6    "married": True,
 7    "divorced": False,
 8    "children": ("Lisa","Jim"),
 9    "pets": None,
10    "cars": [
11      {"model": "BMW 230", "mpg": 27.5},
```

```
12        {"model": "Ford Edge", "mpg": 24.1}
13    ]
14  }
15
16  print(json.dumps(x))
```

Section 28.4 - Format the Result

The example above prints a JSON string, but it is not very easy to read, with no indentations and line breaks.

The json.dumps() method has parameters to make it easier to read the result:

Example:

Use the indent parameter to define the numbers of indents:

```
1  json.dumps(x, indent=4)
```

You can also define the separators, default value is (", ", ": "), which means using a comma and a space to separate each object, and a colon and a space to separate keys from values:

Example:

Use the separators parameter to change the default separator:

```
1  json.dumps(x, indent=4, separators=(". ", " = "))
```

Section 28.5 - Order the Result

The json.dumps() method has parameters to order the keys in the result:

Example:

Use the sort_keys parameter to specify if the result should be sorted or not:

```
1  json.dumps(x, indent=4, sort_keys=True)
```

Python Try Except

The `try` block lets you test a block of code for errors.

The `except` block lets you handle the error.

The `else` block lets you execute code when there is no error.

The `finally` block lets you execute code, regardless of the result of the try- and except blocks.

Section 29.1 - Exception Handling

When an error occurs, or exception as we call it, Python will normally stop and generate an error message.

These exceptions can be handled using the `try` statement:

Example:
The `try` block will generate an exception, because x is not defined:

```
1  try:
2    print(x)
3  except:
4    print("An exception occurred")
```

Since the try block raises an error, the except block will be executed.

Without the try block, the program will crash and raise an error:

Example:
This statement will raise an error, because x is not defined:

```
1  print(x)
```

Section 29.2 - Many Exceptions

You can define as many exception blocks as you want, e.g. if you want to execute a special block of code for a special kind of error:

Example:
Print one message if the try block raises a `NameError` and another for other errors:

167

```
1  try:
2    print(x)
3  except NameError:
4    print("Variable x is not defined")
5  except:
6    print("Something else went wrong")
```

Section 29.3 - Else

You can use the `else` keyword to define a block of code to be executed if no errors were raised:

> **Example:**
>
> In this example, the `try` block does not generate any error:

```
1  try:
2    print("Hello")
3  except:
4    print("Something went wrong")
5  else:
6    print("Nothing went wrong")
```

Section 29.4 - Finally

The `finally` block, if specified, will be executed regardless if the try block raises an error or not.

> **Example:**

```
1  try:
2    print(x)
3  except:
4    print("Something went wrong")
5  finally:
6    print("The 'try except' is finished")
```

This can be useful to close objects and clean up resources:

> **Example:**
>
> Try to open and write to a file that is not writable:

```
1   try:
2     f = open("demofile.txt")
3     try:
4       f.write("Lorum Ipsum")
5     except:
6       print("Something went wrong when writing to the file")
7     finally:
8       f.close()
9   except:
10    print("Something went wrong when opening the file")
```

The program can continue, without leaving the file object open.

Section 29.5 - Raise an exception

As a Python developer you can choose to throw an exception if a condition occurs.

To throw (or raise) an exception, use the `raise` keyword.

Example:
Raise an error and stop the program if x is lower than 0:

```
1   x = -1
2
3   if x < 0:
4     raise Exception("Sorry, no numbers below zero")
```

The `raise` keyword is used to raise an exception.

You can define what kind of error to raise, and the text to print to the user.

Example:
Raise a `TypeError` if x is not an integer:

```
1   x = "hello"
2
3   if not type(x) is int:
4     raise TypeError("Only integers are allowed")
```

Python User Input

Section 30.1 - Python User Input

Python allows for user input.

That means we are able to ask the user for input.

The method is a bit different in Python 3.6 than Python 2.7.

Python 3.6 uses the input() method.

Python 2.7 uses the raw_input() method.

The following example asks for the username, and when you entered the username, it gets printed on the screen:

Python 3.6

```
1  username = input("Enter username:")
2  print("Username is: " + username)
```

Python 2.7

```
1  username = raw_input("Enter username:")
2  print("Username is: " + username)
```

Python stops executing when it comes to the input() function, and continues when the user has given some input.

Python String Formatting

To make sure a string will display as expected, we can format the result with the `format()` method.

Section 31.1 - String `format()`

The `format()` method allows you to format selected parts of a string.

Sometimes there are parts of a text that you do not control, maybe they come from a database, or user input?

To control such values, add placeholders (curly brackets {}) in the text, and run the values through the `format()` method:

Example:

Add a placeholder where you want to display the price:

```
1  price = 49
2  txt = "The price is {} dollars"
3  print(txt.format(price))
```

You can add parameters inside the curly brackets to specify how to convert the value:

Example:

Format the price to be displayed as a number with two decimals:

```
1  txt = "The price is {:.2f} dollars"
```

Section 31.2 - Multiple Values

If you want to use more values, just add more values to the `format()` method:

```
1  print(txt.format(price, itemno, count))
```

And add more placeholders:

Example:

173

```
1   quantity = 3
2   itemno = 567
3   price = 49
4   myorder = "I want {} pieces of item number {} for {:.2f} dollars."
5   print(myorder.format(quantity, itemno, price))
```

Section 31.3 - Index Numbers

You can use index numbers (a number inside the curly brackets {0}) to be sure the values are placed in the correct placeholders:

Example:

```
1   quantity = 3
2   itemno = 567
3   price = 49
4   myorder = "I want {0} pieces of item number {1} for {2:.2f} dollars."
5   print(myorder.format(quantity, itemno, price))
```

Also, if you want to refer to the same value more than once, use the index number:

Example:

```
1   age = 30
2   name = "Harrison"
3   txt = "His name is {1}. {1} is {0} years old."
4   print(txt.format(age, name))
```

Section 31.4 - Named Indexes

You can also use named indexes by entering a name inside the curly brackets {carname}, but then you must use names when you pass the parameter values txt.format(carname = "Ford"):

Example:

```
1  myorder = "I have a {carname}, it is a {model}."
2  print(myorder.format(carname = "Ford", model = "Mustang"))
```

Python File Open

File handling is an important part of any web application.

Python has several functions for creating, reading, updating, and deleting files.

Section 32.1 - File Handling

The key function for working with files in Python is the open() function.

The open() function takes two parameters; *filename*, and *mode*.

There are four different methods (modes) for opening a file:

```
1  "r" - Read - Default value. Opens a file for reading, error if the file does not exi\
2  st
3
4  "a" - Append - Opens a file for appending, creates the file if it does not exist
5
6  "w" - Write - Opens a file for writing, creates the file if it does not exist
7
8  "x" - Create - Creates the specified file, returns an error if the file exists
```

In addition you can specify if the file should be handled as binary or text mode:

```
1  "t" - Text - Default value. Text mode
2
3  "b" - Binary - Binary mode (e.g. images)
```

Section 32.2 - Syntax

To open a file for reading it is enough to specify the name of the file:

```
1  f = open("demofile.txt")
```

The code above is the same as:

```
1   f = open("demofile.txt", "rt")
```

Because "r" for read, and "t" for text are the default values, you do not need to specify them.

Note: Make sure the file exists, or else you will get an error.

Python File Open

Section 33.1 - Open a File on the Server

Assume we have the following file, located in the same folder as Python:

demofile.txt

```
1   Hello! Welcome to demofile.txt
2   This file is for testing purposes.
3   Good Luck!
```

To open the file, use the built-in open() function.

The open() function returns a file object, which has a read() method for reading the content of the file:

Example:

```
1   f = open("demofile.txt", "r")
2   print(f.read())
```

If the file is located in a different location, you will have to specify the file path, like this:

Example:

Open a file on a different location:

```
1   f = open("D:\\myfiles\welcome.txt", "r")
2   print(f.read())
```

Section 33.2 - Read Only Parts of the File

By default the read() method returns the whole text, but you can also specify how many characters you want to return:

Example:

Return the 5 first characters of the file:

```
1  f = open("demofile.txt", "r")
2  print(f.read(5))
```

Section 33.3 - Read Lines

You can return one line by using the `readline()` method:

Example:

Read one line of the file:

```
1  f = open("demofile.txt", "r")
2  print(f.readline())
```

By calling `readline()` two times, you can read the two first lines:

Example:

Read two lines of the file:

```
1  f = open("demofile.txt", "r")
2  print(f.readline())
3  print(f.readline())
```

By looping through the lines of the file, you can read the whole file, line by line:

Example:

Loop through the file line by line:

```
1  f = open("demofile.txt", "r")
2  for x in f:
3    print(x)
```

Section 33.4 - Close Files

It is a good practice to always close the file when you are done with it.

Example:

Close the file when you are finish with it:

```
1  f = open("demofile.txt", "r")
2  print(f.readline())
3  f.close()
```

Note: You should always close your files, in some cases, due to buffering, changes made to a file may not show until you close the file.

Python File Write

Section 34.1 - Write to an Existing File

To write to an existing file, you must add a parameter to the open() function:

"a" - Append - will append to the end of the file

"w" - Write - will overwrite any existing content

Example:

Open the file "demofile2.txt" and append content to the file:

```python
1  f = open("demofile2.txt", "a")
2  f.write("Now the file has more content!")
3  f.close()
4
5  # open and read the file after the appending:
6  f = open("demofile2.txt", "r")
7  print(f.read())
```

Example:

Open the file "demofile3.txt" and overwrite the content:

```python
1  f = open("demofile3.txt", "w")
2  f.write("Woops! I have deleted the content!")
3  f.close()
4
5  # open and read the file after the overwriting:
6  f = open("demofile3.txt", "r")
7  print(f.read())
```

Note: the "w" method will overwrite the entire file.

183

Section 34.2 - Create a New File

To create a new file in Python, use the open() method, with one of the following parameters:

"x" - Create - will create a file, returns an error if the file exist

"a" - Append - will create a file if the specified file does not exist

"w" - Write - will create a file if the specified file does not exist

Example:

Create a file called "myfile.txt":

```
1  f = open("myfile.txt", "x")
```

Result: a new empty file is created!

Example:

Create a new file if it does not exist:

```
1  f = open("myfile.txt", "w")
```

Python Delete File

Section 35.1 - Delete a File

To delete a file, you must import the OS module, and run its `os.remove()` function:

Example:
Remove the file "demofile.txt":

```
1  import os
2  os.remove("demofile.txt")
```

Section 35.2 - Check if File exist:

To avoid getting an error, you might want to check if the file exists before you try to delete it:

Example:
Check if file exists, *then* delete it:

```
1  import os
2  if os.path.exists("demofile.txt"):
3    os.remove("demofile.txt")
4  else:
5    print("The file does not exist")
```

Section 35.3 - Delete Folder

To delete an entire folder, use the `os.rmdir()` method:

Example:
Remove the folder "myfolder":

```
1  import os
2  os.rmdir("myfolder")
```

Note: You can only remove *empty* folders.